365 DAYS of BABY LOVE

Playing, Growing and Exploring with Babies
from Birth to Age 2

by Sheila Ellison and Susan Ferdinandi

Sourcebooks Inc.

Naperville, IL

Published by: **Sourcebooks, Inc.**
P.O. Box 372, Naperville, Illinois 60566
(630) 961-3900
FAX: (630) 961-2168

Rhymes from *Father Gander Nursery Rhymes* reprinted with permission.
© Copyright 1985 by Dr. Douglas W. Larche, published by Advocacy Press, P.O. Box 236, Santa Barbara, CA 93102

Ellison, Sheila.
    365 days of baby love / by Sheila Ellison and Susan Ferdinandi.
        p.   cm.
    ISBN 1-57071-110-0 (pbk.): $12.95
    1. Infants—Miscellanea.   2. Infants—Care—Miscellanea.   3. Parenting—Miscellanea.
4. Play—Miscellanea.   5. Creative activities and seat work—Miscellanea.
I. Ferdinandi, Susan.   II. Title.
HQ774.E485   1996
649'.122 — dc20
                                                                    96-33707
                                                                         CIP

Printed and bound in the United States of America.

Acknowledgments

To my sister and co-author Sheila Ellison for her generous encouragement and guidance throughout the writing of this book.

—Susan

To my children Brooke and Rhett for eagerly illustrating, and giving me their ideas, and to Wesley, who not only illustrated, but blacklined more illustrations than I did. To my parents Nancy and Dave Maley for all their "Grandparenting" time. And, a special thanks to Bryan Hidalgo for proofreading, editing, and continual creative support.

—Sheila

The authors wish to extend a sincere thank you to all the children who illustrated this book, and to their teachers, Robin Toews and Ardath Kroner, who let us come into their classrooms to draw.

Dedication

To my five year old son Troy for teaching
me that any difficulty can be overcome. For
inspiring me each day with his new words,
his courage, and his willingness to live life to
its fullest, even when it's a challenge.

—Sheila Ellison

To my husband Dale and my children Dillon and
Elizabeth. Thank you for all the baby days.

—Susan Ferdinandi

INTRODUCTION

We believe that the magic of childhood lies in the everyday moments. From birth through two years old, most moments are spent caring for, teaching, holding, and growing through baby's first experiences. There are so many things baby learns to do in such a short time that sometimes we blink and a stage is gone. This book will give you ideas of ways to spend magical time together. Included are sections on floor time, language and sound, nature, art, music, movement, family growth, grandparenting, parks and recreation, water-play, siblings, baby's room, and everyday toys.

Each section starts with infant-appropriate activities and progresses up through two year olds. Since age doesn't dictate ability, try things out and see what your baby likes and can do. The best way for you to understand your baby is to observe, so pay attention to baby's growing personality. Babies bring joy, they teach life. What a wonderful gift!

Sheila Ellison

Susan Dickinson

Wit & Wisdom

The advice in the Wit & Wisdom sections of this book was given to us by parents from across the country who wanted to pass on their tricks, tips, baby secrets, and wisdom to you. We would like to thank them for sharing their experiences with us. We're always looking for good advice to be added to future editions, so write to us at Sourcebooks.

Table of Contents

1 Caregiving

1 ....Bonding
2 ....What, Another Diaper!
3 ....How Sweet It Is
4 ....Safe to Explore
5 ....When Baby Grabs the Spoon
6 ....Baby's Right to Cry
7 ....Look Before You Leap
8 ....The Choice Is Yours
9 ....The Gift of Gab
10 ....Is Baby Ready?
11 ....Bathroom Exploration
12 ....Getting Dressed
13 ....Daily Routine

2 Language and Sound

14 ....Gurgles and Coos
15 ....Pa-Ba-Da-Ba
16 ....Baker's Baby
17 ....More Piggy Toes
18 ....Baby Face
19 ....Give Me
20 ....Instant Replay
21 ....Picture This
22 ....Playful Rhymes for Joyful Times
23 ....Nose, Eyes, Hands
24 ....Uh-oh, It's the Giant!
25 ....Tippy Toe
26 ....Baby's Poem
27 ....Who Says MOOO?
28 ....More Than Words
29 ....Where Game
30 ....Big or Little
31 ....Telephone Talk

3 Bedtime

32 ....Together Time
33 ....Rock a Baby
34 ....Bedtime Ritual
35 ....Kiss Me Game
36 ....Tape a Story
37 ....Imaginary Friend Stories
38 ....Peace Hug
39 ....Imagine
40 ....Baby Won't Sleep
41 ....Dream Pillow
42 ....Teeth Brushing
43 ....Bedtime Chart

4 Baby's Room

44 ....Allergy Free
45 ....Safety Tips
46 ....Wall Mural
47 ....Blackboard
48 ....Photo Wallpaper
49 ....Penny Wish Container
50 ....Colored Light
51 ....What's Hanging?
52 ....Baby's Box
53 ....Colored Jar Storage
54 ....Rotating Art Display
55 ....Friends and Family
56 ....Display Shelf
57 ....Permanent Photo

5 Writing Exercises

58 ..... Your Child's Journal
59 ..... No Time for Problems
60 ..... Birthday Letter
61 ..... Baby's Phrases
62 ..... Positive Feelings
63 ..... What's in a Name?
64 ..... Fantasy Day
65 ..... Your Journal
66 ..... Letter to Yourself
67 ..... Life Story
68 ..... Day Dream
69 ..... Letter of Thanks

6 Movement

70 ..... Daily Walk
71 ..... Massage
72 ..... Morning Exercise
73 ..... Stretching
74 ..... Wiggle Worms
75 ..... Dancing the Night Away
76 ..... Baby Flying
77 ..... Scarf Shuffle
78 ..... Learn to Climb
79 ..... Mirror Dance
80 ..... Shake Dance
81 ..... Go Get It
82 ..... Rope Shapes
83 ..... My Little Locomotor

7 Music

84 ... Song with Baby's Name
85 ..... Self-Made Songs
86 ..... Shake and Rattle
87 ..... Your Child's Voice
88 ..... Foot and Hand Jingles
89 ..... Guess the Noise
90 ..... Music Is Hiding
91 ..... Rhythm Sticks
92 ..... Song of Humor
93 ..... Rubber Band Harp
94 ..... Bongo Drums
95 ..... Louder, Softer Please
96 ..... Finger Tapping
97 ..... Story Sound Effects

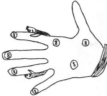

8 Everyday Toys

98 ..... Black and White Pictures
99 ..... Mobiles
100 ..... Textured Touch
101 ..... Pictures to Chew
102 ..... Discovery Rattle
103 ..... Floor Roller
104 ..... Personal Picture Book
105 ..... Finger Puppets
106 ..... Clothespin Fun
107 ..... Stringing Box
108 ... Golf Tee Hammer Box
109 ..... Bead Catcher
110 ..... Paper Balls
111 ..... Kitchen Boxes

9 Floor Time

112	Magic Mirror
113	Welcome to My World
114	Box of Socks
115	Fill and Roll
116	Crawl Space Race
117	Cheerio!
118	Magic Act
119	Wrap It Up!
120	Bouncing Cupcakes
121	My Beautiful Balloon
122	Stack Attack
123	Make Me a Match
124	Twisting and Turning
125	Tub of Delights
126	Tube Slide
127	Soft Ball Socks
128	See Saw

10 Art

129	The Art's in the Doing
130	Contact Collage
131	Crumple Crazy
132	Fingers, Hands, and Elbows Too
133	Musical Chalk
134	Sandpaper Line Designs
135	A Box Is a Box
136	The Scribble
137	Moving Masterpiece
138	Shapes
139	Potato Prints
140	Foil with Oil
141	Color Search
142	Stained Glass Window
143	Blob Painting
144	Watercolor
145	Rubber Stamp Art

11 Nature

146	Meet the Animals
147	Special Tree
148	Sky's the Limit
149	Feel the Wind
150	Bird Watch
151	What's That Smell?
152	Plant a Seed
153	Nature Museum Display
154	Sand Cake
155	Centerpiece
156	Moon Watch
157	Bug Trap
158	Tree and Leaf Rubbings
159	Egg Head
160	Wish on a Star
161	Sunrise
162	Nature Walk

12 Dramatic Play

163	Mr. Moon
164	Horsey Ride
165	It's Spider Time
166	Ding-a-Ling
167	Deep Sea Adventure
168	Under the Umbrella
169	Over and Over
170	Finders Keepers
171	Magic Carpet Ride
172	Play Is Hard Work
173	Mountain Bear
174	What If?
175	Jack and Jill Cooperate
176	Dress-Up Box

13 Storytelling

177 .... Moon Glow
178 .... Do I Have One for You
179 .... Young Collector
180 .... Seeing Is Believing
181 .... Moving Story
182 .... All Stuffed Up
183 .... Trip Story
184 .... Draw and Tell
185 .... Collage Story
186 .... Shadow Stories
187 .... Tree Home Stories

14 Clay and Playdough

188 .... Everyday Playdough
189 .... Another Dough, No Cooking Required!
190 .... Puff Dough
191 .... Tea Party Dough
192 .... Gooey Goop
193 .... Super Stretch Dough
194 .... Old Fashioned Fun
195 .... Cornmeal Dough
196 .... Cornstarch Dough
197 .... Clay Works

15 Water Play

198 .... String of Floaters
199 .... Bubbles and Waves
200 .... Learn to Pour
201 .... Pavement Painting
202 .... Dish Washing
203 .... Wiggle Slide
204 .... Rub-a-Dub Scrub
205 .... Bubbles for Baby
206 .... Happy Helper
207 .... Some Float, Some Don't
208 .... Rainbow Surprise
209 .... Freeze for All

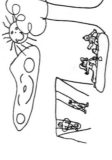

16 Parks and Recreation

210 .... Just Strolling Through
211 .... Breakfast Club
212 .... A Place to Park
213 .... Swing Rhythm
214 .... Ready for Anything
215 .... The Sandbox Scene
216 .... Anticipate Problems
217 .... Tree Love
218 .... Hi Kites
219 .... Tiny Treasure Hunt
220 .... Five, Six, Pick-Up Sticks
221 .... What's Yours Is Mine

17 Celebrations

222 ......Neighborhood Welcome
223 ......Baby Sleeps All Night
224 ......Sibling Party
225 ......Baby's Birthday
226 ......Birthday Theme Ideas
227 ......Pass the Parcel
228 ......Baby Things Exchange Party
229 ......Thanksgiving Box
230 ......Winter Picnic
231 ......Sing Along
232 ......Christmas Morning
233 ......The Way We Were
234 ......Spring Is Here
235 ......Husbands as Servants

18 Family Growth

236 ......Point of View
237 ......Family Journal
238 ......Perfect Imperfection
239 ......Family Postcards
240 ......Teaching Compassion
241 ......Who Are You?
242 ......Do Nothing Day
243 ......Love Letter
244 ......New Traditions
245 ......Memory Lane
246 ......Surprise
247 ......Thirty Minute Talk
248 ......Video Moments
249 ......Play Date
250 ......Play Hooky

19 Mother's Time

251 ......What Is a Mother?
252 ......Tea for You
253 ......Surrender Control
254 ......Vision Poster
255 ......Write It Now
256 ......Role Models
257 ......Fun Time
258 ......Jazz Clean
259 ......Learn It Together
260 ......Buy Flowers
261 ......Special Photo Album
262 ......Time to Organize
263 ......Fast Makeover
264 ......Weekend Escape

20 Dad's Time

265 ......Baby's World
266 ......What Is a Father?
267 ......Another Dad
268 ......Mother and Wife
269 ......Reality to Fantasy
270 ......Dad Things
271 ......Who Are You?
272 ......Box Forts, Tunnels, and Tents
273 ......Alone with Baby
274 ......Junk Mailman
275 ......Shoebox Train
276 ......Talk About Feelings
277 ......Sex After Baby

21 Siblings

278 .....You Are Great!
279 .....A Picture of Me
280 .....Child's Photo Album
281 .....A Hero's Story
282 .....Big Brother and Sister Shirts
283 .....How I Feel
284 .....Puppet Theater
285 .....Nature Collage
286 .....Homemade Picture Book
287 .....Handprint Cookies
288 .....Scavenger Hunt
289 .....Ring of Love
290 .....Layered Bottle Art
291 .....Food Fair
292 .....Where's Your Bottle?

22 Grandparenting

293 .....What Do You Need?
294 .....Meet the Neighborhood
295 .....Food for Thought
296 .....Establish a Play Area
297 .....Baby's Memories
298 .....Excursions
299 .....Traditions
300 .....Photo Opportunity
301 .....Individual Attention
302 .....Life on Tape
303 .....Plant a Garden
304 .....Special Books
305 .....Picture Frame
306 .....Grandma's Jewelry Box
307 .....Lullaby Lane

23 On the Go

308 .....Travel Tips
309 .....Where to Go
310 .....Restaurant Tips
311 .....Napkin Art
312 .....Grocery Store Game
313 .....Bring a Shoe
314 .....Spyglass Necklace
315 .....Touch Adventure
316 .....Out and About
317 .....I Spy
318 .....Silly Photo
319 .....Have a Conversation
320 .....Edible Necklace
321 .....Count Together

24 Baby-sitting and Playgroups

322 .....Organizing a Playgroup
323 .....Playgroup Leader's Responsibilities
324 .....Parent Questionnaire
325 .....Co-op Baby-Sitting
326 .....Hiring a Baby-Sitter
327 .....What Can Babies Do?
328 .....Calm Down
329 .....Toy Parade
330 .....Little Rabbit Foo Foo
331 .....Circle Time
332 .....Bean Bag Games
333 .....Obstacle Course
334 .....Freeze Frame
335 .....Common Games
336 .....Saying Good-Bye

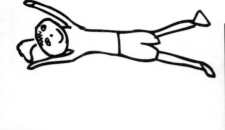

25 Food and Nutrition

337 ....Apricot and
                Apple Puree
338 ....Vegetable Puree
339 ....Vegetable Custard
340 ....Corn Cereal
341 ....Yogurt Plus
342 ....Chocolate Dipped
                Fruit
343 ....Egg in a Bun
344 ....Baked Bread
                Sandwiches

345 ....Grandma's Granola
346 ....Cheese Pretzels
347 ....Designer Pancakes
348 ....Honey Lover's
                Chicken
349 ....Time Saving Trifle
350 ....Ice Cream Cone
                Cakes
351 ....Gift Wrapped
                Sandwiches

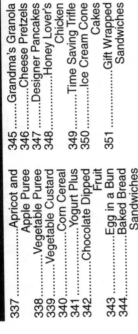

26 Development

352 ....The First Two Months,
                Big and Small Muscles
353 ....The First Two Months,
                Express and Think
354 ....Three to Five Months,
                Big and Small Muscles
355 ....Three to Five Months,
                Express and Think
356 ....Six to Eight Months,
                Big and Small Muscles
357 ....Six to Eight Months,
                Express and Think
358 ....Nine to Eleven Months,
                Big and Small Muscles

359 ....Nine to Eleven Months,
                Express and Think
360 ....Twelve to Seventeen Months,
                Big and Small Muscles
361 ....Twelve to Seventeen Months,
                Express and Think
362 ....Eighteen to Twenty-Four Months,
                Big and Small Muscles
363 ....Eighteen to Twenty-Four Months,
                Express and Think
364 ....Two Years Old,
                Big and Small Muscles
365 ....Two Years Old,
                Express and Think

Caregiving

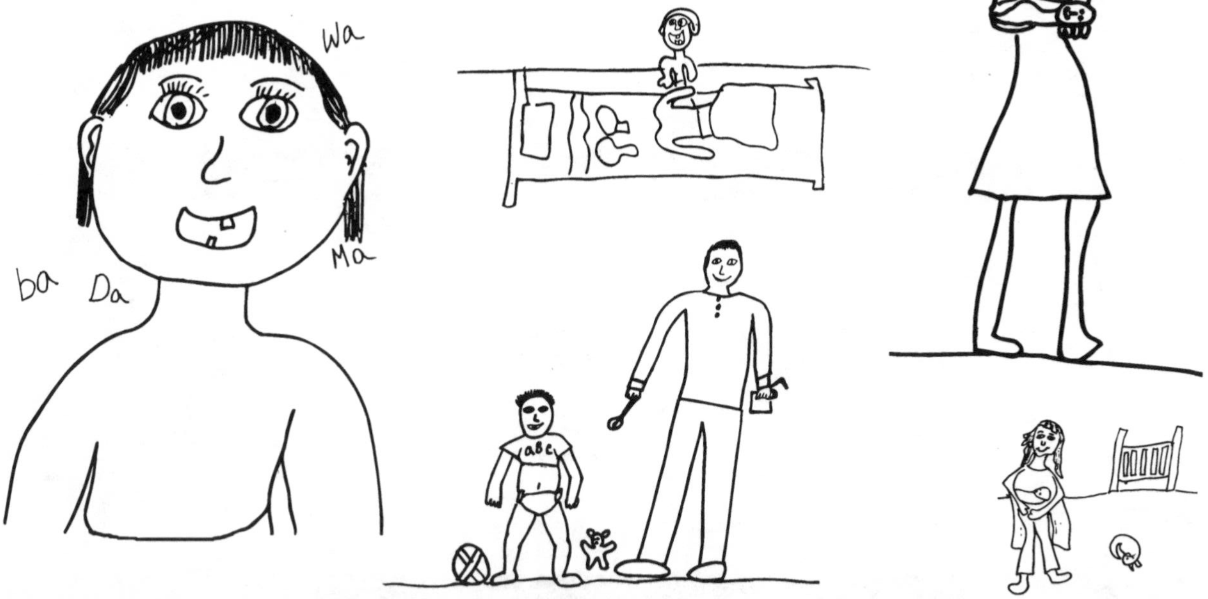

Bonding

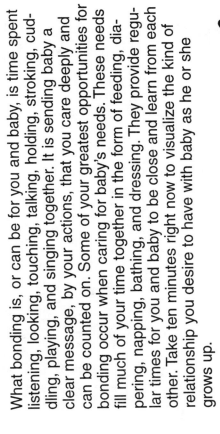

What bonding is, or can be for you and baby, is time spent listening, looking, touching, talking, holding, stroking, cuddling, playing, and singing together. It is sending baby a clear message, by your actions, that you care deeply and can be counted on. Some of your greatest opportunities for bonding occur when caring for baby's needs. These needs fill much of your time together in the form of feeding, diapering, napping, bathing, and dressing. They provide regular times for you and baby to be close and learn from each other. Take ten minutes right now to visualize the kind of relationship you desire to have with baby as he or she grows up.

What, Another Diaper!

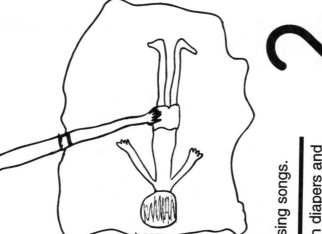

2

Include baby while diapering by talking about what you are doing. Show baby what is going on. This invites baby's participation and encourages communication. One of the best ways to involve baby is by lovingly talking to him or her: say, "I'm going to change your diaper," "Here is your wet diaper," "You help me when you hold still." Observe the subtle ways baby responds. Your calm voice and gentle touch teach baby to trust the new world into which they've just recently arrived. Diapering is a perfect time to gently massage baby's feet, stomach, back, face, or hands. It is also a good time to say rhymes and sing songs.

Wit & Wisdom: Many new moms are back to using cloth diapers and rubber pants. To keep rubber pants soft, add vegetable oil to the wash.

—Glenda A., Newton, IL

How Sweet It Is

3

Whether baby is nursed, bottlefed, or both, feeding times are precious because of the physical closeness and warmth you share. Baby will study your face very carefully, seeking eye contact with you. Better to relax and drink in that shining face than sit calculating how many ounces baby has consumed. When baby holds your finger or thumb, gently wiggle it around and tell baby, "I feel your little hand," "you're holding my finger." Does baby's grip tighten or change as you speak? Do this little relaxation exercise while you are nursing: starting with your toes, tense the muscles then relax; move up your body tensing every muscle for a few seconds, then consciously relaxing it. This is also a great exercise to do before bed if you have a hard time falling asleep.

Wit & Wisdom: When you take baby from the crib or cradle in the middle of the night, place a heating pad in the empty crib so when the feeding is over baby can return to a warm, cozy bed.
—Elaine W., Boston, MA

Safe to Explore

Although movement is limited during the first few months of life, it is still possible for baby to wiggle and turn herself into potential danger. Check all areas of a room baby might be able to squirm, wiggle, roll, or scoot to. Never leave baby alone on a high surface. Get down on the floor and check for things that baby could pull on, crawl into, crawl under, chew and swallow, squeeze, and throw.

- Cover electrical outlets.
- Cover all heaters.
- Protect baby from windows and mirrors that are not shatterproof.
- Tie up all drapery cords and any kind of string.
- Get rid of slippery throw rugs.
- Get rid of poisonous plants or put them far out of reach (most common house plants are poisonous).

- Cribs and other furniture for baby must meet consumer protection safety standards. Also, the crib mattress must fit snugly so baby can't get stuck between mattress and side of crib and smother.
- Keep all medicines and cleaning materials out of baby's reach.
- Do not buy toys with small parts that can come off and be swallowed by baby.
- Make sure all toys and materials are non-toxic.
- Keep a first-aid kit and learn baby CPR.
- Make sure emergency phone numbers are by the phone.

When Baby Grabs the Spoon

Take baby grabbing the spoon as a sign that he wants to feed himself, or at least try! Here are some ideas to help make this transition successful:

- Use unbreakable, child-size utensils.
- Offer finger food: small pieces of soft food that baby can pick up, such as bananas.
- Small quantities of food are better than overwhelming baby with "family style" servings. Baby can always have more and there won't be as much mess to clean up.
- Allow time for play and experimentation, but be aware of your own limits regarding how food is handled.
- Self feeding is most successful in a relaxed atmosphere. There's nothing like having your face wiped with a sponge every time cereal drops on your chin to take the fun out of eating.

- When baby stops eating, end the meal and clear baby's place—unless you want to see whatever is left smeared over everything within reach!

Wit & Wisdom: When my son Julian was beginning to eat, I would put a standing mirror in front of him so he could see himself. He loved watching himself eat and I think he learned more quickly how to hold the spoon.
—*Liliana Kochanek, Hendersonville, TN*

5

Baby's Right to Cry

6

Baby's cry can evoke a wide range of feelings in those who hear it: worry, fear, frustration, anger, and sadness. When baby cries, try your best to find out why by listening, looking, and feeling for the answer. Once you've exhausted all the possibilities: wet, hungry, hot, cold, bored, tired, lonely, feverish, or other visible physical symptoms (and called your pediatrician if you believe the problem is medical), you've done your best. You will not always discover why baby is crying, and that's OK. Ask baby why they're crying and leave space for baby to respond. Setting up this two-way communication even before baby speaks recognizable words is very important, establishing a healthful pattern for your growing relationship. When baby cries and you don't understand why, hold baby, or place baby in a crib, or on a cozy blanket on the floor. Close your eyes, take several deep breaths exhaling slowly, and remember, crying is part of being alive and being human.

Look Before You Leap

Look before you leap into solving baby's dilemmas (unless the situation is dangerous), and identify what baby is trying to do. Support and encourage baby's effort, but allow baby to do what he or she is capable of doing. Help with tasks that prove too frustrating. One situation might be that baby crawls under a coffee table and starts to cry. Instead of running over and pulling baby out, involve baby by lying down on the floor and talking about the situation, "I see you're stuck under here," then gently guide baby out. Episodes like this will happen often and are real learning experiences in problem-solving.

Wit & Wisdom: If you are getting confused which breast you fed baby from last, put a ring on one of your fingers and, after you feed, switch it to the side you will feed baby from next.

—*Elizabeth P., Jacksonville, FL*

The Choice Is Yours

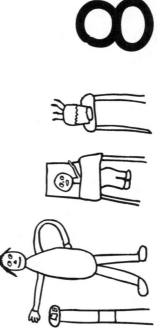

Baby can learn to be a participating, responsible member of your family—and eventually society—but it doesn't happen automatically. Whenever possible, give baby real choices by weaving opportunities for choice-making into your daily routines together. For instance, at meal time ask baby, "Do you want bread or crackers?" "Are you thirsty for water or milk?" When dressing, encourage baby to "choose between the blue shirt or yellow shirt." Say, "you can wear these sweatpants or this jumper." If there are several pairs of pants or shorts from which to choose, let baby make the choice. Of course sometimes there is no choice, so don't offer one.

Wit & Wisdom: Don't let the medical profession make you doubt yourself. I learned long ago that doctors aren't always right. Look long and hard to find doctors you feel will listen to you.
—*Sandy Welsh, Galesburg, IL*

8

The Gift of Gab

Oh, how thrilling to hear baby's words come trickling out—first one, then three, then two and three word sentences! Now more than ever, speak clearly and directly to baby. Use fewer words, such as, "let's wash hands, it's dinner time," instead of, "It's time to wash your hands because we're going to be eating dinner in about five minutes." When baby talks to you, respond and add to what was said. Baby might say, "Daddy eat," and you repeat, "yes, Daddy is going to eat" or "Daddy will eat with us."

Wit & Wisdom: When I had a newborn, I could never find time to shower. I was too afraid of not being able to see her every waking moment. My neighbor suggested I buy a see-through shower curtain.

—*Eva T., Chicago, IL*

Is Baby Ready?

Baby will want to use the toilet eventually, because that is what everyone else does. The question is when. Baby will use the toilet when:

- They are physically ready, meaning they are able to control muscles of the body involved in this task. They must be able to hold on and let go when necessary.
- They are mentally ready, meaning they know what is expected of them.
- They are emotionally ready, meaning they want to do it.

Ideas for stress-free toilet training:

- Make toilet easy to get on and off so baby's independence is encouraged.
- Dress baby in clothes that are easy for baby to remove.
- A gentle, understanding response is helpful when accidents happen.
- Tension and anger will spoil your best efforts, and could make toilet training a lengthy and negative experience for everyone.

Wit & Wisdom: Put several drops of either red, green, or blue food coloring in the potty before they go. They will be so excited to see it change color that they will look forward to doing it again.

—Dawn P., West Palm Beach, FL

10

Bathroom Exploration

Spend some time exploring the bathroom with baby. Show how different objects found in the bathroom are used. Show baby how they work together: like a toothbrush and toothpaste, hairbrush and hair, sponge and soap, etc. Wet baby's hands and dry them with a towel. Fill up the bathtub a little and talk about how the drain holds water in, then lets it out. Flush the toilet a few times. Remember, even if baby is not able to ask questions, they are still wondering.

Wit & Wisdom: As baby begins to use the toilet, use baby wipes instead of toilet paper.

—Howard V., Exeter, NH

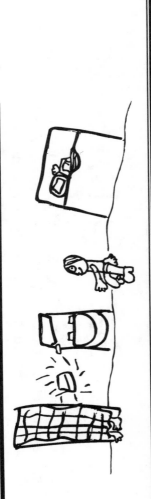

11

Getting Dressed

While you are getting dressed, have a little fun teaching baby the names of clothes: socks, shoes, tee-shirt, pants, sweatshirt, dress. Put two articles of clothing out on the floor next to baby and say, "baby touch the (clothing)." Wait a moment for baby to respond, then say, "let's put the (clothing) on!" Replace the article of clothing with another and repeat until baby is dressed. Baby might like playing this game with your clothes as well.

Wit & Wisdom: Amanda loved our dressing game each morning. I would put each piece of clothing on halfway then let her finish it up. She liked being part of a team, and I think she was satisfied that she was doing part of it herself.

—Susan K., Cedarburg, WI

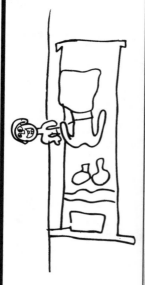

Daily Routine

Babies love routine. If you can get some sort of routine going, your life will be easier and baby will know what to expect. It is a good idea to plan your daily routine around what baby already does. For the next three days, write down when baby eats and sleeps. After a few days, you might see a pattern developing. Decide on times close to baby's patterned times and follow through for a week eating or sleeping at those times. Fit other daily activities in between these planned times. This gives you time to schedule other things and it makes caretaking easier.

Language and Sound

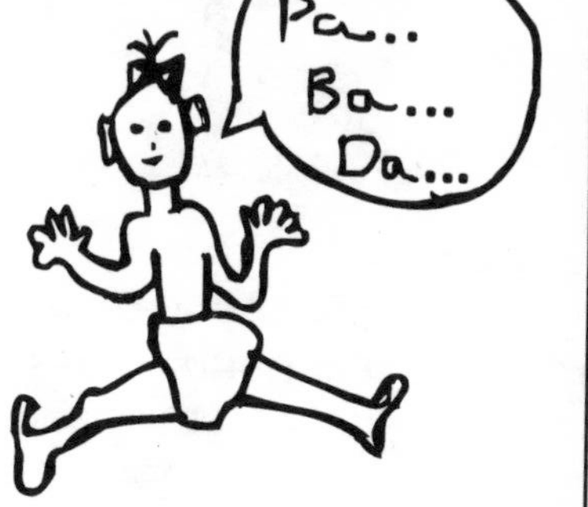

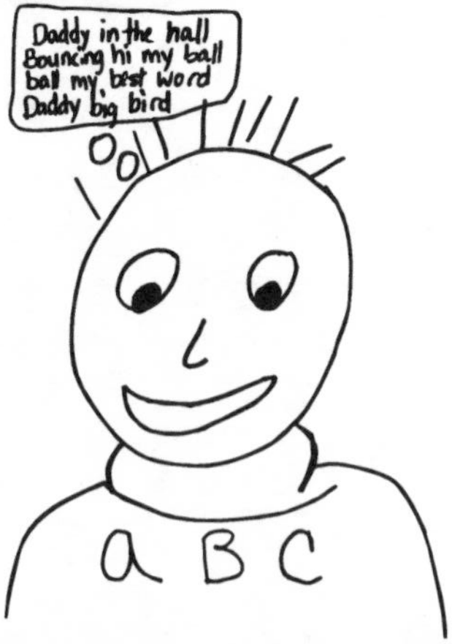

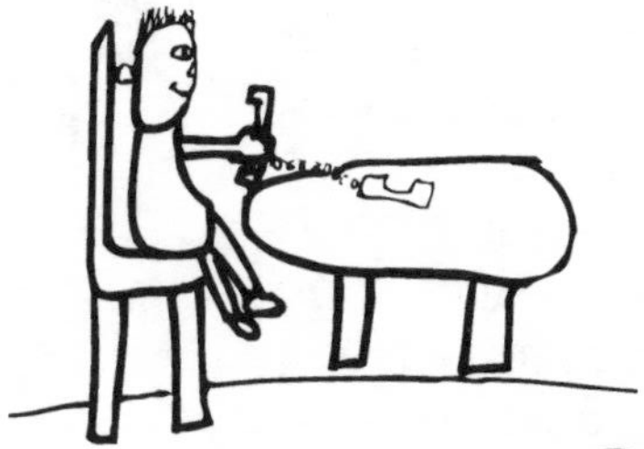

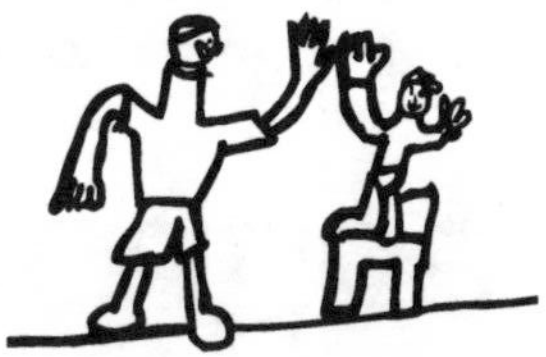

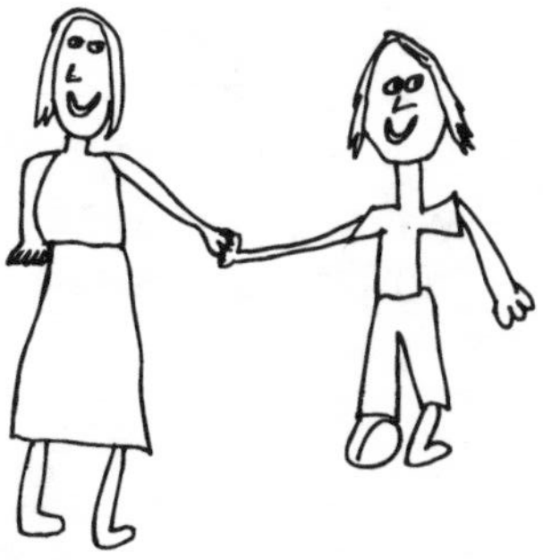

Gurgles and Coos

14

Lie down next to baby on a comfortable surface like a carpeted floor or bed. Start making babbling sounds: ma, ba, da, etc. When baby makes babbling sounds back, respond by looking into baby's eyes, rubbing baby's tummy, and smiling a big smile. Repeat the sounds baby just made and wait for baby to respond with more sounds. Rub baby's tummy and smile. Congratulations! You just had your first conversation.

Wit & Wisdom: Every stuffed animal my daughter received as a gift was named using the last name of the person who gave it to her. She now has a lasting relationship with these people through her animal friends.

—*Mary Jane W., Grafton, WI*

Pa-Ba-Da-Ba

As baby grows, his or her ability to vocalize new sounds increases, especially if they have been spoken and sung to by a sensitive caregiver. When baby engages you in conversation by making sounds, repeat the sound back to baby in a familiar word; for example, baby says "pa," and you say "Papa," ba...bottle, ma...mama, be...baby, and so on. Older siblings are good at coming up with creative words. Baby reaches out in many ways to communicate. Paying attention and responding encourages language development.

15

Baker's Baby

Set baby on your lap facing you. As you hold baby's hands, gently make that cake together.

Pat-a-cake, pat-a-cake baker's man
(clap hands together)
Bake me a cake as fast as you can
Roll 'em and roll 'em and mark 'em with a B
(roll hands around and trace letter on baby's hand)
And toss 'em in the oven for baby and me.
(point to baby, then yourself)

Lie baby on back and repeat using baby's feet. Repeat this many times if baby approves.

16

More Piggy Toes

Here's a chance to play with those adorable, tiny feet. Hold baby's big toe gently between your thumb and index finger and say:

This little piggy went to market. (big toe)
This little piggy stayed home. (second toe)
This little piggy had roast beef. (third toe, eggplant may be substituted for vegetarians)
This little piggy had none. (fourth toe)
This little piggy cried wee, wee, wee all the way home. (fifth toe)

As you say "wee, wee, wee," walk fingers up baby's leg, across tummy, and up to chin and lightly tickle.

17

Baby Face

Materials
A favorite doll or stuffed animal

Sit or lie comfortably with baby. Touch baby's head, eyes, ears, nose, and chin, naming each part as you sing the following song to the tune of "Here We Go Round the Mulberry Bush":

This is what I call my head,
Call my head, call my head.
This is what I call my head,
Listen, look, and see.

Now I know the parts of me,
Parts of me, parts of me.
Now I know the parts of me,
Listen, look, and see.
(repeat, adding other body parts)

An older baby would enjoy pointing to the parts on a doll, stuffed animal, or you as the song is sung.

18

Give Me

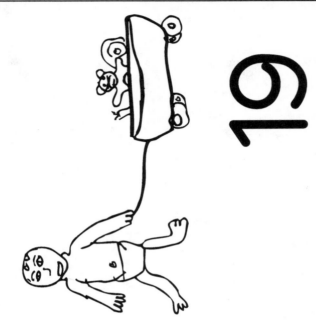

This game can be played anywhere. It teaches baby what the words "give me" mean, as well as introducing baby to the concept of sharing an object without losing it. Sit facing baby. Find an interesting toy to hand to baby and, as you do, say, "(your name) is giving baby the (object name)." Let baby look at the toy and play with it a bit as you use descriptive words to talk about the toy. Then say, "baby give (your name) the (object name)," hold out your hand, say thank you, and smile as baby hands it to you. Repeat with other toys. As baby gets older, you can make it more fun and a bit harder by saying, "give me a yellow toy," or "give me a small doll," letting baby go and find what you asked for.

Instant Replay

Materials
Tape recorder
Blank cassette tape

Record baby's sounds and the conversations you have together. Play them back and observe baby's response. Some babies become quite animated and vocalize, while others become quite still. Older babies may want to push the buttons of the recorder. Have fun with this, and remember, most recorders are built to withstand the pressure of curious little hands.

20

Picture This

Materials
Magazines, picture books, catalogues

Sit with baby on your lap as you turn the pages of a book or magazine. Point out and name objects baby might recognize. Say things like, "see the baby," "look at the dog," "the bike is red." What does baby like to look at? As you go about everyday activities, name things in baby's world: chair, table, bed, stove, lamp, window, rug. What better way to learn that everything has a name than from the voice baby loves the most—yours!

Playful Rhymes for Joyful Times

Be creative when it comes to nursery rhymes.
These have evolved over many years, and will
continue to do so for many more. Use baby's
name in places, or change pronouns to match
baby's gender. Oh, and feel free to make them
politically correct, we won't tell.

Thumbkin, Pointer, Middleman-big,
(point to baby's fingers one at a time)
Silly Man, Wee Man,
Rig-a-jig-jig.
(roll baby's hands around each other)
(Traditional, England)

Bumblebee was in the barn
(circle one finger in the air by baby)
Carrying dinner under his arm.
(move finger closer to baby)
Buzzzzzzzzz (poke baby gently)
(Traditional, United States)

One, two, three,
(bounce baby gently on your knee or in
your arms)
Baby's on my knee.
Rooster crows and
(Say Cock-a-doodle-doo!)
Away baby goooooooes!
(lower your knees toward the floor, keeping
firm hold of baby)
(Traditional, United States)

Nose, Eyes, Hands

Pick one body part to focus on for an entire day, such as hands. Sing songs about hands, point hands out in story-books, on people, pets, television, etc. Take baby on a walk around the house, pointing to hands wherever you see them. Wiggle, wave, clap, or shake your hands. Do the same for nose, ears, feet, etc., using the following ideas: breathe through your nose and let baby feel the air or hum and let baby feel your nose vibrate; listen to each other's heartbeat; dance with your feet, or lie on your backs and wiggle them in the air; talk about or make noises with your teeth, tongue, and lips, blow air out, whistle, make popping sounds with your lips, open and close your mouth. The options are endless, so have fun.

Wit & Wisdom: My kids love sand. I found that a little cornstarch on a piece of cloth is a gentle way of rubbing off all the sand from hands and feet before climbing into a clean car or marching into the house.

—*Holly S., Minnetonka, MN*

23

Uh-oh, It's the Giant!

These two action rhymes are fun to do when baby has begun to babble long and short groups of sounds, such as tatata, bibibi, dada, etc. They are short, repetitive, and include several sounds already or soon to be in baby's repertoire.

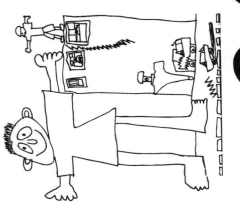

Fee Fi Fo Fum - Here's my fingers, here's my thumb. (Wave fingers then thumb)
Fee Fi Fo Fum - Fingers gone, so is thumb. (Curl four fingers into fist, then thumb follows)

Repeat this by replacing the F in Fee Fi Fo Fum with B, T, D, and M.

24

Tippy Toe

Tippy Tippy Tiptoe, off we go.
Tippy Tippy Tiptoe, to and fro.
Tippy Tippy Tiptoe, through the house.
Tippy Tippy Tiptoe, quiet as a mouse.

Use your fingers to "tiptoe" up baby's arm, over head, and down the other arm. Tiptoeing around the house while holding baby and whispering the words is another way for baby to experience your voice. If you're both walking, baby might enjoy leading you around as you say the rhyme together.

25

Baby's Poem

As baby grows and begins to recognize words for everyday things, such as cup, baby, juice, bottle, mama, daddy, etc., and has one or two words to say, then it's time to compose a poem. Let the whole family get involved using baby's own words, and those baby recognizes, to create a heartwarming ditty sure to leave everyone smiling.

Wit & Wisdom: My daughter hated to wear hats. Because she had fair skin, she had no choice. One day, I decided to put a hat rack up for her and buy a few different sun hats. I hung it in her room and now that she gets to choose one each day, she gladly wears them.

—Silvia T., Daytona, FL

Daddy in the hall
Bouncing hi my ball
ball my best word
Daddy big bird

a B C

oo

Who Says MOOO?

Collect pictures of different animals from magazines, postcards, stickers, cards, and posters. Old calendars are a great buy in stores at year-end and have large colorful pictures of many animals baby is certain to know. Look at the animal pictures with baby. Spread them on the floor around you and play WHO SAYS _____? (fill in blank with animal sounds). OK, some animals are extremely quiet or make sounds that are virtually impossible for humans to imitate, but try anyway! Ask baby to bring you the picture. Use color, size, and shape words to describe animals too.

More Than Words

Baby soon realizes that words have meaning and are connected to specific actions. These two rhymes contain many action words baby is beginning to understand.

*Two Little Blackbirds (you and baby are
the blackbirds)
Sitting on a hill (couch, chair, or low stool).
One named Jack (point to baby).
And one named Jill (point to yourself).
Fly away Jack (baby pretends to fly away
behind couch or chair).
Fly away Jill (you fly away and join baby).
Come back Jack (both fly back to original
spot).
Come back Jill.*
(Traditional, England)

*Humpty Dumpty sat on a wall
Humpty Dumpty had a great fall.
All of the horses, the women and men
Put Humpty Dumpty together again.*

Reprinted with permission from "Father Gander Nursery Rhymes," by Dr. Douglas W. Larche, published by Advocacy Press.

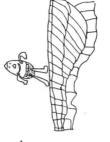

Where Game

Hold baby and ask *where* questions like: Where is baby's bed? Where is baby's nose? Where is mommy's room? When baby is very small and doesn't know how to point, he may simply look in that direction. Walk where baby looks and say, "there is baby's bed!" Even if baby doesn't seem to know, answer each question yourself, going toward the object you asked about. When baby is older they will point themselves, and later they will run to show you.

Wit & Wisdom: I never seemed to get enough water when I was nursing, especially in the middle of the night since I was too tired to walk to the kitchen. I found a great solution: I fill a water bottle with ice and water before I go to bed and place it next to my baby's bed.

—Lyn H., Reno, NV

29

Big or Little

Collect different sizes of the same types of objects for baby to arrange by size. They could be shoes, boxes, shells, stones, books, silverware, toys, blocks, bowls, and balls. In each group of objects, ask baby to choose the big _____, then the small _____. If there are more than two of an object, encourage baby to arrange them in order from biggest to smallest. Baby might decide to create an arrangement with all the objects that has nothing to do with size, but pleases baby immensely. Respect baby's hard work.

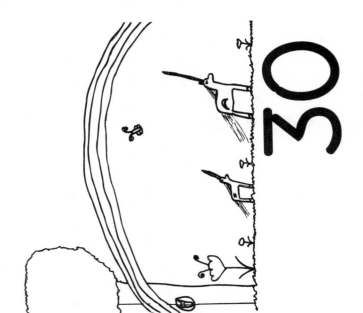

30

Telephone Talk

Materials
2 play telephones

Instead of getting baby one play telephone, get two, so baby can have real conversations with you. At first you will just be babbling to each other, taking turns of course, but later baby will begin to copy how you talk on the phone. What better way to begin to learn the rules of conversation?

Wit & Wisdom: Whenever I clean the house, I give my son a big soft bristle paintbrush to sweep up the crumbs.

—Rita B., Scottsdale, AZ

31

Bedtime

Things To Do
Pick up
Toys

Together Time

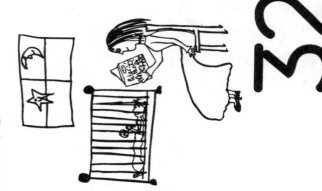

Pick one hour each night, about the time baby goes to bed, and make a rule: no phone calls or visitors during that hour. That way you can peacefully put baby to bed without being interrupted or distracted. Once baby is in bed, you will hopefully be left with at least 15 minutes to talk as a couple, able to give each other your complete attention. Once the hour is up, you can go on with life as usual. This action is a constant reminder that family matters.

Wit & Wisdom: Every night about an hour before my kids are supposed to go to bed I start whispering. It seems to calm the whole house down.

—Ashley T., La Honda, CA

32

Rock a Baby

Baby will love your voice no matter how it sounds, so don't eliminate singing based on your own self-critical view of your voice. Sing lullabies to baby that will soothe both of you. If you don't know any, buy a lullaby tape and memorize a few. Rock together, holding baby close as you sing softly. Here is one to try:

Sleep, Baby, Sleep
*Sleep, baby, sleep, thy father guards the
    sheep.
Thy mother shakes the dreamland tree,
and from it fall sweet dreams for thee.
Sleep, baby, sleep.*

*Smile, baby, smile, thy mother guards
    awhile.
Thy father tends the dreamland tree, and
    shakes a new sweet dream for thee.
Smile, baby, smile.*

Reprinted with permission from "Father Gander Nursery Rhymes," by Dr. Douglas W. Larche, published by Advocacy Press.

33

Bedtime Ritual

A bedtime ritual is something you do before bedtime that is the same every night. Routine is important for a child's sense of security. It also makes the actual transition into bedtime go smoother since your child knows that you will follow through and actually put them in bed. Here is an example: bathe for 15 minutes, have a snack, read or tell a story, talk about what baby did that day and what they will do tomorrow, say a short prayer or meditation softly, or sing a lullaby. Even if you have to shorten each stage, try to stick to your plan and bedtime will be a breeze.

Author's Note: One of the most beautiful tapes of original lullabies we have found is entitled "From a Mother's Heart," by Liliana Kochanek. The lyrics all deal with concepts such as love and self-esteem, and the melodies are gorgeous. Contact ArtPeace Music, 194 Cherokee Road, Hendersonville, TN 37075, (800) 500-0649.

Kiss Me Game

35

This game teaches body parts at the same time as you touch and bond with each other. Start with a nose kiss, that is, rubbing your noses together, move to your chins and rub them together, your foreheads, ears, eyes, eyelashes, hair, and so on. Don't forget feet, elbows, knees, and stomach. Baby will giggle with delight and will ask to carry out this tradition each night, and still be asking you for various "kisses" when they are five!

Wit & Wisdom: The best thing I ever put in my son's room was a spare twin mattress placed on the floor. When he was a baby it made a great reading corner, and as he grew, it had many uses: for tumbling, wrestling, bouncing, fort construction, etc.

—Brian T., St. Cloud, MN

Tape a Story

36

Materials
Tape recorder
Blank cassette tape
Child's favorite storybook

Make a cassette tape to play each night as baby goes to sleep. Record songs, poems, stories, or anything else baby likes. The important thing is for baby to hear your familiar voice. This is also perfect for the times baby goes to Grandma and Grandpa's, to a baby-sitter, or when you are out of town.

Wit & Wisdom: Before I go to bed each night, I put a few quiet time activities in a special basket for my two year old to do when she wakes up in the morning. I usually get a little extra sleep!

—*George W., Milwaukee, WI*

Imaginary Friend Stories

Bedtime is the perfect time to tell made-up stories. Without pictures to look at, your child is more likely to close his eyes, relax, and interact with you. Early on, make up a character that is the child's same age and sex. The character goes to all sorts of interesting places, ones that your child shows interest in: birthday parties, school, camping, the ballet, zoo, etc. Make up a new adventure each night. Your child will look forward nightly to this time together. There is something extra special about stories made up by you!

Wit & Wisdom: I needed a rug for the nursery so I purchased a piece of remnant carpet about 10 foot by 10 foot. I then found some large number and letter stencils and spray painted them onto the rug. We have made up numerous games, and my son loves to run and touch whatever number or letter I call out.

—*Elaine B., Bellevue, WA*

37

Peace Hug

38

A peace hug is when you hold baby long enough so that YOU relax completely, letting all your tensions dissolve as you breathe. When you are very tense it may take five minutes to relax, so hold on until you feel peace wash over you. Feel baby breathing and breathe with him. This hug works wonders if you have just lost your temper over something your child has done. Better yet, instead of losing your temper in the first place, try a peace hug.

Wit & Wisdom: "We cannot start too early in giving a child continuous, warm, consistent affection. He simply must have this unconditional love to cope most effectively in today's world."

—Dr. Ross Campbell

Imagine

When children are falling asleep, a peaceful state is at hand. This is the time to tell them an "Imagine" story. It is different from a regular story. You are going to merely suggest what direction the child's mind goes, letting them wander around in their own thoughts a bit. This could be called a guided meditation. When a baby is small, you could start telling stories each night about a special place they might be familiar with, like a garden, meadow, or grove of trees. Describe this place slowly in a soft voice and in great detail. Tell them to try to see this place in their mind. Talk about the friendly animals, a wise person or guardian angel, and a large rock where they can leave their worries. Make up all sorts of stories using this setting. When baby is old enough to follow the story, you will lead them into their special place

through your words, then leave them on their own in silence for a few minutes to interact and imagine. As you lead them out of their place, talk about how their good feelings will go with them, and that whenever they want to visit this place, they can in their own mind. Be creative and try to incorporate any problem areas you see. For example, if they are afraid of people, bring some people into the scene and talk about all the fun they are having together.

39

Baby Won't Sleep

What can you do when baby won't sleep through the night? First of all, there are many books written on this subject and they support many different theories. Here are a few points to try to remember:

- Babies rarely sleep through the night before three months, and after that, through the night usually means from midnight to 6 a.m.

- Start observing why baby is waking up. Are they hungry or do they just want to see you?

- Wait five minutes after you hear baby before you rush into their room—see if they will fall back to sleep by themselves. Babies wake up all through the night and if you run in at every sound they will get used to it and expect it.

- If baby is 6 months to a year old and still not sleeping through the night, you may have to let them cry for a few minutes, then go in and pat them on the back. Make sure they are OK, but don't take them out of bed or feed them. It may also help if dad goes in to see baby instead of mom. Do this for a few nights. Then, don't go in every time and see if they will go back to sleep themselves.

- If you are very frustrated with sleep problems, get help from your pediatrician.

40

Dream Pillow

Materials
White pillowcase
Fabric paint (non-toxic)
Piece of cardboard

Make a good dream pillow. Before you start painting, put the piece of cardboard in between the pillowcase. Draw an angel, a teddy bear, a picture of mom, dad, brothers, and sisters or whatever you think baby would recognize and like on the pillowcase. This pillowcase can travel wherever baby goes. It's an easy way to bring baby's secure feelings to wherever he or she sleeps.

Wit & Wisdom: My daughter loves to take off her clothes, so to keep her from taking off her one piece pajamas, I cut off the feet and turned them backwards. Now she can't reach the zipper.

—Clara W., San Jose, CA

Teeth Brushing

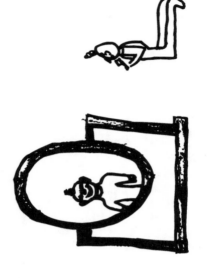

When babies are just getting teeth, give them a toothbrush to chew on. As they begin to brush their teeth with your help, here are a few ideas to make them like it more:

- Talk to their teeth, make up a running story as you brush. Ask them to open their mouth wide so you can see the characters you are talking about.
- Let baby brush your teeth after you have brushed theirs.
- Give them a small flashlight and let them look at your teeth. This might generate interest in the subject.

Wit & Wisdom: If you live in a cold place and want to prevent your baby from catching a chill, take a shower yourself first, then bathe the baby when the room is warm from the steam.

—*Nicole T., Portland, OR*

42

Bedtime Chart

Make a chart with drawn pictures of the things baby does each night that lead up to bedtime. You may even want to take real pictures and put them up on the chart. It's fun for baby to go up to the pictures and know what to do next without being told. This is especially evident around two years old when baby wants to be more independent. Make sure to give lots of smiles and hugs as each step is completed.

Wit & Wisdom: I bought a gardener's pad to put on the floor next to the bath. Now I can kneel on the floor for as long as my baby wants to splash and gurgle.

—Angela T., Niles, IL

Things To Do
Pick Up
Toys

43

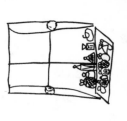

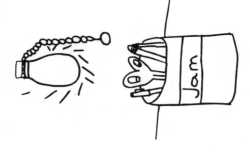

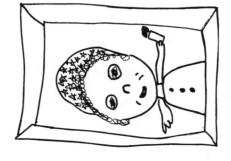

Baby's Room

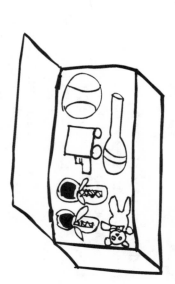

Allergy Free

If allergies run in your family, here are a few things you can do to minimize suffering in the baby's room:

1. Encase mattress in a dustproof, plastic, zip-shut mattress bag. Call an allergist's office and ask them for a recommended company to buy the bag from.
2. Avoid upholstered furniture.
3. Choose synthetic materials rather than natural fibers, a polyester-filled pillow rather than feathers, nylon carpet instead of wool, etc. Sheets and blankets can be cotton if washed frequently (the house dust mite is a common allergen and it lives off natural fibers).
4. Have only washable stuffed animals and wash them once a month.
5. Have hardwood floors if possible, using throw rugs on top that can be washed.
6. Keep surfaces clear so they can be dusted or vacuumed two to three times per week.
7. Keep all pets with fur, hair, or feathers out of baby's room.

Safety Tips

- Keep baby's bed free of long ribbons, cords, or hanging toys that baby might reach.
- Keep lamp and appliance cords out of reach so that baby can't tug or chew on them.
- As soon as baby can crawl, cover unused electrical outlets with safety caps.
- Screen off unguarded heaters.
- Keep crib and playpen away from windows so baby can't pull down curtains or crawl out the window.
- Don't put any climbable objects near windows.
- Store toys and games low, and dangerous objects high and out of reach or locked up.
- Position hanging hooks well above child's eye level.

- Remove small objects baby could choke on from the house.
- Check any paint suspected of being used before 1978 for lead poisoning.
- Install smoke detectors, and if baby's room is on the second floor, purchase one of the rope ladders now available through children's catalogues.
- For baby products that have warnings or recalls, call the Consumer Product Safety Commission at 1-800-638-2772.

Wall Mural

Materials
Overhead projector (borrow one from
    school or local library)
Plastic overhead sheet
Black overhead marker
Picture of mural to be painted on wall
Acrylic paint-tubes (bought at art supply
    stores)
Paintbrushes

Look through picture books or at greeting cards for ideas of pictures, characters, or scenery to paint as a mural on the wall. Decide which wall to put the mural on. Put the plastic sheet over the picture you wish to paint on the wall and trace it with the black marker. Turn on the overhead projector and place the plastic sheet on top.

Move the overhead projector around until the image is shining on the wall in the position you want. You may have to move the machine forward or backward to get the image size you want. Using a pencil, trace the overhead projected lines onto the wall. Turn off the projector and paint in the colors with acrylic paint. Use a black paint pen to do the outline after all the colored acrylic paint has dried.

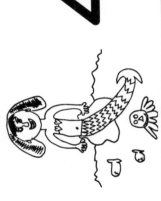

Blackboard

Materials
Blackboard paint
Any surface that is hard and smooth (closet door, bed headboard, wall, particle board)
Paintbrush
Fine sandpaper
Paint cleaner to wash brush

If the hard surface already has some sort of paint on it, you will need to sand the surface until it feels a bit rough, as this helps the blackboard paint to "stick" better. Apply two to three coats of blackboard paint following paint instructions on the can. Once the paint has dried thoroughly, your little artist may begin. Keep a plastic container of colored chalk nearby. An old damp rag works best as an eraser because it easily removes chalk without hard rubbing.

Photo Wallpaper

Materials

Photos of baby and family   Piece of yarn and nail
Wallpaper paste and brush   Clear gel acrylic
Clean rag

This designer wallpaper is made out of photocopied pictures glued to the wall. The results are wonderful! Choose ten black and white photos you like and have the negatives made into 5 x 7 or 8 x 10 black and white prints. Take the prints to a copy store and copy the photos onto sheets of paper. Measure the size of the wall you plan to cover with the pictures to decide how many copies of each picture will be needed. Decide on a pattern to follow. Tie a nail to a piece of yarn. Tape the yarn to the upper edge of the wall so the yarn will hang in a straight line. Once the yarn is hanging straight, tape it to the bottom of the wall. Follow this line when putting up the first row of pictures. Put wallpaper paste on the wall, then put one paper picture up at a time, rubbing over the top with a clean rag to make sure there are no bubbles. Continue in this way until all pictures are on the wall. Once the wall is dry, paint at least two coats of a gel acrylic over the top of the paper.

48

Penny Wish Container

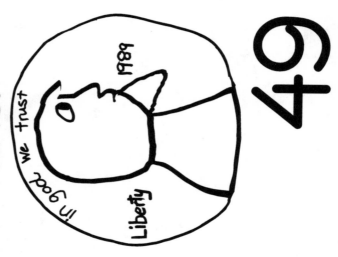

Materials
Pretty glass container
Lots of pennies

Whenever a friend or family member comes to visit, ask them to make a penny wish for baby and put it in the special container in baby's room. Keep up this custom as baby grows and one day you will be able to explain to them that many people have wished good things for their life, and that they have always been loved. The tradition could continue throughout life, maybe once a year on their birthday. No matter where they live or how old they are you can send them a penny wish!

Colored Light

Materials
Glass jars of all sizes with lids
Food coloring

This is a great way to introduce baby to colors. First, fill the jars with water. Add a few drops of food coloring to each jar, experimenting with the amount of color. Then mix the colors so all the colors of the rainbow can be represented. Put the lids on the jars and arrange them on a windowsill near baby's crib. When the sunlight shines through the window, beautiful patterns of light will be seen.

red + yellow = orange
red + blue = purple
blue + yellow = green

What's Hanging?

Materials
Ceiling hook used for hanging plants
Yarn or string
Things to hang: scarves, party or holiday decorations, small figures, stuffed animals, balloons, etc.

Attach ceiling hook into the ceiling directly above baby's bed. Tie the string securely to whatever object is being hung. Lower the object so it hangs 7 to 9 inches from baby's face. The lighter objects like scarves and ribbons will move as a breeze or fan hits them and will interest baby for a longer period of time than objects that hang still. Change your objects daily, leaving the string attached, then store them in a box or container. After a few days use the same object again. Newborn to about six week old babies will just look at the objects. When baby begins to reach up and grab at the objects, make very sure they are tied on securely. Don't hang anything that could hurt baby if it is pulled down.

Baby's Box

Create a special box to keep all baby's treasures until they become adults and it's time for them to leave home. It could be a wooden box or a cardboard box. Whatever you choose, make it special. Put in baby's first pair of shoes, clothing worn home from the hospital, first hair cut, a cassette tape with first noises and words, hand and footprints, special cards written to baby, a small picture album, first drawing, etc. The box will hold all of baby's treasures throughout their life, so be sure to make it a big box!

Colored Jar Storage

Materials
Many glass baby food jars
Paint
Contact cement
Shelf

Paint the inside of the lids of the baby food jars to match baby's room colors. Glue the jar lids to the underside of a shelf with the contact cement. Let the lids dry overnight, then screw the jars onto the lids. Use jars for storage of small things or put interesting and colorful things in the jar for baby to look at while they are being changed.

Rotating Art Display

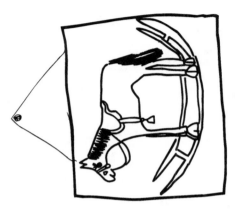

Materials
Plastic poster frames
Homemade art work

Find a place on baby's walls to hang the plastic frames. In the beginning, put paintings or drawings from siblings in the frames. When baby produces his or her first work of art, place it in the frame. Change the pictures within the frames weekly to display all incoming masterpieces. Keep this up as baby grows. Depending what the frame is like, you may be able to store the artwork on top of each other within the frame, creating a safe, out-of-the way scrapbook of sorts.

Wit & Wisdom: Use snap-on plastic shower curtain hooks to attach toys to the crib, stroller, or car seat.
—*Allen M., Wichita, KS*

54

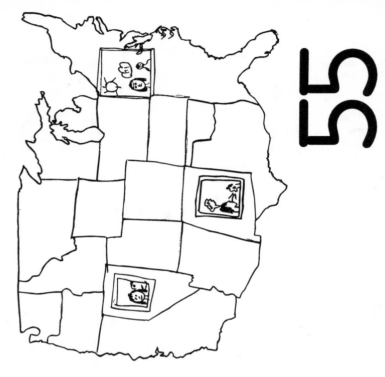

Friends and Family

Materials
United States or World map
Pictures of family and friends
Lightweight paper or foam frames
Stick pins or double-sided tape

Put the map up on baby's wall. Glue the pictures into the frames and hang them on the map according to where friends and family live. Point to the pictures regularly, telling baby about people and places. It is also fun to make some sort of mark on the map on the places baby visits along with the date of travel.

Display Shelf

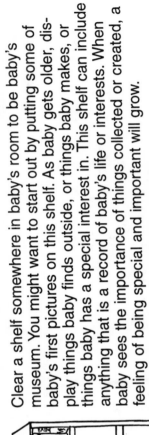

Clear a shelf somewhere in baby's room to be baby's museum. You might want to start out by putting some of baby's first pictures on this shelf. As baby gets older, display things baby finds outside, or things baby makes, or things baby has a special interest in. This shelf can include anything that is a record of baby's life or interests. When baby sees the importance of things collected or created, a feeling of being special and important will grow.

Wit & Wisdom: I created a stuffed animal hammock out of an old sheet. Fold it into a triangle, tack one point into the corner, and the other points to the side walls.

—Gabby Crescini, Santa Clara, CA

Permanent Photo

Materials
Buy a frame to hold a school-size photo for each child in the family.

Put a current photo of each child in individual frames. Each year put a new and current photo over the top of the old one. Keep putting the new photos over the old, letting the frame serve as storage for past years' treasures.

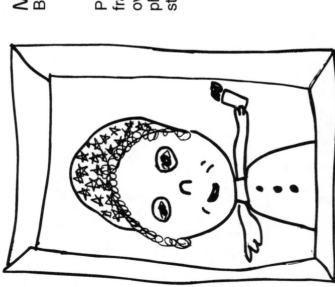

Writing Exercises

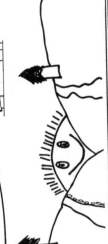

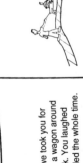

Today, we took you for a ride in a wagon around the block. You laughed and smiled the whole time.

HAPPY Birthday

Your Child's Journal

Buy a blank book and start writing to your child today. Your child may not be born or your child may be three years old; whatever the age, it is never too late to begin recording your thoughts, feelings, observations, and descriptions of your child's life and personality. Write as often as you can and include your feelings about the child, how they contribute to the beauty of your life, and most of all your feelings of love. Write letters to them to record things you want them to know when they are adults that you might forget over time. As your child grows and changes, read them some of your words when they are going through hard times, or when they think you hate them because you need to correct their behavior. It will remind them that you have been loving them for a long time, you have been there with them, and will continue to love them no matter what. When your child leaves home, give them the journal. This might be the gift your child will cherish most from you.

Today, we took you for a ride in a wagon around the block. You laughed and smiled the whole time.

58

No Time for Problems

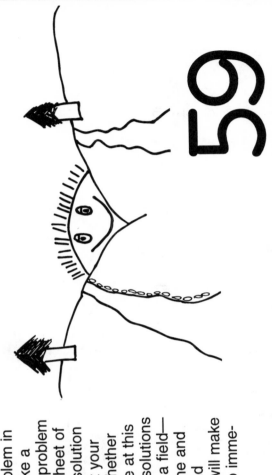

59

Parents are usually too busy to solve problems, they just live through them! Pick a problem in your life. Be brave and take a minute to write down the problem in the middle of a blank sheet of paper. Brainstorm every solution you can think of. Don't let your solutions be judged by whether or not they seem possible at this time. Your brainstorming solutions are like seeds planted in a field—one will take root over time and begin to grow. Feeling and expressing the problem will make you feel better, even if no immediate solution is at hand.

Birthday Letter

Write a birthday letter to your baby every year. It doesn't matter if you have missed one, two, or five. What will matter is that on baby's 18th birthday you can hand her letters written about life, about her babyhood, and about how much you loved, supported, and encouraged her. So often as parents we think we will remember everything, but we don't. Be sure to read the letters over or make copies before you give them away.

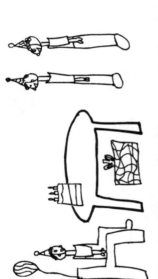

60

Baby's Phrases

Get a special, very small, blank, hard-covered book of some sort. Carry it with you so you won't forget to write down baby's words. Of course not every word is worthy of writing, but the word combinations that make you smile are the ones you won't want to forget. Make sure you write some pronunciation code so you remember the the actual sound of the words as baby said them.

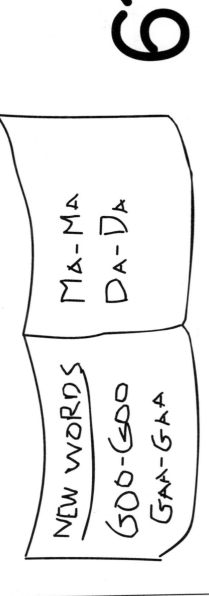

Positive Feelings

Do you ever feel tired enough that you don't want to get out of bed? Or maybe you feel sad about some aspect of your life. On index cards, write down positive, happy, uplifting thoughts of your own, or quotes by others. Read them when you wake up in the morning. Read them before you go to bed at night. Read them when you feel tired or sad. It helps to write down positive affirmations in areas of your life you might be working on. It's a way of retraining your brain. For example, if you are not a morning person and you dislike getting out of bed in the morning, the affirmation might read, "I will wake up bright and ready to face the morning with energy and happiness." It's possible this could be called brainwashing, but it works!

What's in a Name?

When your baby grows up to be five or six years old, they will definitely want to know why you chose the name you did for them, what other names you thought of, and why you didn't choose one of those names. So keep one step ahead of them and write it down! Write the list of names and your thoughts on each one. Most importantly, write your baby's chosen name with as much information as you can find: what the name means, country of origin, etc. If baby is named after someone, include personal information on that person.

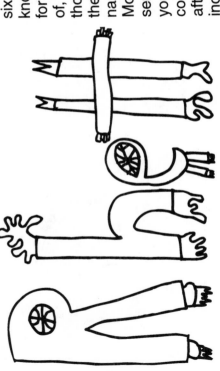

63

Fantasy Day

New parents have little time for leisure, so here's a way to sneak a fantasy day into thirty minutes! First, write down your fantasy day in detail from morning to night. Everything must go the way YOU want it to. Maybe you wake up in the morning to a day with nothing to do but read. Do you spend the day scuba diving from a beautiful yacht? Do you envision yourself lounging on a tropical island? Is your fantasy a day when everyone in your life treats you like a queen? Hope and dream big, and remember, this is a fantasy! When you finish writing, close your eyes and visualize in clear detail yourself going through your fantasy day.

Your Journal

Writing thoughts and feelings down in a special book that only you read is called journalizing. It is amazing what pearls of insight can be gained by this simple reflection. Buy a blank book today and begin writing. When you look back every few months, growth will be obvious! Write everything you think, fear, dream, or wonder. If you need to make a decision, write about it— your own advice will surprise you.

65

Letter to Yourself

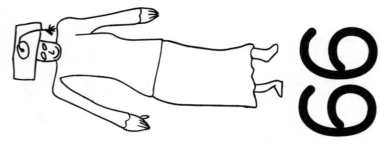

Sometimes when moms and dads get caught up in daily duties like caregiving and work they lose sight of the larger picture of their lives. Seeing the larger picture means being able to see the present day as part of a whole lifetime. Take a few minutes today and write a letter. The letter will be from your 20 year old child written to you. Start the letter like this:

Dear Mom and Dad,
I learned so many thing from you about life . . . .
During the hardest parts of my life you . . . .
When I didn't know what decisions to make . . . .

Add whatever you want to this letter, date it, and keep it. Shaping and guiding a child is a life's work that merely starts with how you talk to baby on the changing table. What you do, say, and model to your child creates a life. In other words, what you are doing is important work. Remember that the next time you wake up at 4 a.m. to feed or soothe your little darling!

Life Story

We all have a story to tell. What better time than the present to get some of your life memories down on paper? Seeing your children go through similar experiences will remind you of your own childhood. Also, parents and relatives will be more likely to tell you stories about yourself after you have your own children. You don't have to be a great writer to write your life story. All you need to do is try to remember, and be as honest as possible with your feelings. In fact, as baby grows, these experiences from your life will make great short stories that they may ask you to repeat many times.

Day Dream

In your journal or on a blank sheet of paper, begin to write the dreams you have for your life. Put everything you can think of into it no matter how out of reach they seem. You may want to divide the page into categories: personal, children, marriage, career, material possessions, etc. The important thing is not to restrict your dream writing in any way. Do this every few months and keep them. Would you be surprised to see your dreams developing into reality?

Wit & Wisdom: Someone once told me something when I was thinking of going back to college to get a master's degree. She said that I should first write down what I wanted out of my life, then decide if I needed a master's degree to achieve it. That person saved me years of education I didn't need.

—*Angela M., Hartford, CT*

Letter of Thanks

Throughout life there have been people who have guided, supported, loved, encouraged, and lead you. Take time today to think of someone from your childhood who helped shape you into the person you are. Remember what qualities they had. Write them a letter telling them about yourself today, about your family, about the goals and dreams you accomplished, and most importantly, how they helped you grow into who you are. It's so important to support the positive in our world; so often, we remember the hurt but forget the positive. Tell this person you found a hero in them.

69

Movement

Daily Walk

Take at least a fifteen minute brisk walk each day. The fresh air will improve your state of mind as well as exercise your heart. This walk should be a time to breathe, think, and relax. If baby is little and in a carrier in front, the rocking movement of your step will resemble the feeling of being inside your belly, so they will most likely fall asleep. Once baby is bigger, make sure to use a stroller to save your back. Baby will exercise his or her neck trying to see everything that passes by!

Massage

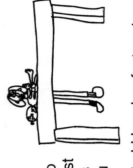

Materials
Blanket or towel
Pure vegetable oil
Soft music (optional)

Make sure the room is warm before beginning. Sit with your back against a couch, with legs stretched straight in front. Place a towel on top of your legs, then put baby on top of the towel. You may need to put a small pillow from knee to foot so baby isn't sliding downward. Now, take baby's clothes off, leaving diaper on if necessary. Pour a small amount of oil into your hand, about the size of a quarter. Rub your hands together until the oil and your hands feel warm. Talk to baby as you gently but firmly place your hands palms down on

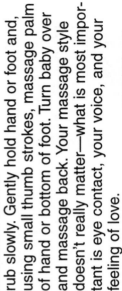

baby's chest. Rub from chest down to toes and from chest out to fingertips as many times as you like. Make sure to rub slowly. Gently hold hand or foot and, using small thumb strokes, massage palm of hand or bottom of foot. Turn baby over and massage back. Your massage style doesn't really matter—what is most important is eye contact, your voice, and your feeling of love.

Morning Exercise

Take time to do some simple exercises together. You may be getting more exercise than baby, but after all, baby has a whole lifetime to get in shape!

- Baby lies on floor on stomach, adult lies on stomach face to face with baby. Adult does push up and as adult goes up baby exercises neck muscles by raising head to look.
- Adult lies on side to do leg lifts. Baby lies on back in front of adult. As adult lifts leg, adult puts hand on baby's stomach and moves baby side to side in a rolling motion.
- Adult lies on back to do stomach curls. Baby lies on adult's chest, stomach to stomach. Adult slowly raises up and down, tightening stomach muscles. Baby enjoys the ride up and down.
- Adult sits in straddle position with baby lying on back between legs. Let baby grasp index finger or thumb with her hands, then let baby pull up slowly, being careful not to let baby fall backwards. As baby lies back down, adult stretches forward.

Wit & Wisdom: I found that my baby could be included in all sorts of exercise. In fact, just lying on the ground, he found it amusing to watch me huff and puff, jump up and down, and grunt a little. I never was able to do an hour straight, but 15 minutes here and there relieved stress and made me feel better about myself.

—*Dana Breen, Portola Valley, CA*

72

Stretching

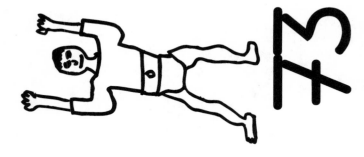

Sit in a comfortable place with baby lying on a flat, soft surface. Sing, talk, or play music baby likes. Hold both of baby's arms out to the side. Grasp the wrists, then gently bring each arm to cross over baby's chest and hold for a few seconds, then return to baby's side. Bend and straighten each arm, then stretch both arms over baby's head. Bend and straighten baby's legs, then touch toes to nose or head. Smile at baby and talk to her about what you are doing. Say, "Stretch, stretch, stretch those cute little legs." Baby loves your voice and may even smile. Stretching is especially important when baby cannot move by herself yet.

Wit & Wisdom: The only time my daughter, who had colic, would stop crying was when I was massaging her. It must have alleviated some of the gas in her stomach.
—*Charlotte H., Washington, DC*

Wiggle Worms

Wiggle wiggle little worm
Crawling through the dirt so warm.
Up through dirt we poke our heads
Looking at our insect friends.
Wiggle wiggle little worm
Wiggle wiggle little worm.

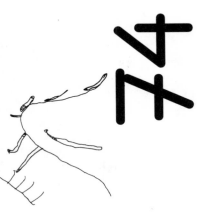

74

Materials
Picture or book about earthworms
Live worm (optional)
Music of any kind

Read a story about worms or look at a live worm. Talk about how worms have no arms or legs so they have to wiggle to get where they want to go. Get down on the floor next to your baby. Hold your arms at your sides and wiggle your body like a worm. Chances are your baby will giggle seeing you do what they have been doing for months in their pre-crawl state! Sing this song to the melody of Twinkle Twinkle Little Star:

Dancing the Night Away

Materials
Your voice
Radio, cassette player, or stereo

Move any object that might trip someone, making enough room to move in all directions.

Everyone can dance, just let yourself go. Hold your baby tight, turn on the music, and just move. Lift baby up and down, turning around and around, lift left and right, step forward and back. If the room isn't large enough, don't confine yourself—move from room to room. This is good exercise for you too!

Baby Flying

As soon as baby can hold his head up, you can play all sorts of flying games. Lie on your back on a bed or floor and, holding baby by the armpits, lift him up and down, side to side, dipping like a plane, and swerving in the air as you make plane sounds. Tell baby they are flying up in the air. Another fun way for baby to fly is to place baby on the floor, stomach down, as you stand above baby with a foot on either side. Hold baby under the stomach and swing back and forth and side to side. Make sure you are bending your knees so you don't hurt your back. Another great swinging game for the older baby (about 9 months) is to take one hand and one foot and swing them around in a circle. You can play this with baby face up or face down. To baby, this truly feels like flying, gliding up and down as they fly around the circle.

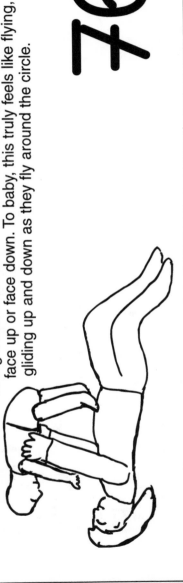

Scarf Scuffle

Materials
Chiffon scarves
Music

Clear any obstacles out of the room or go outside. Give your child a few scarves and begin to throw them into the air. Watch them float down to the ground. Imitate the scarf movements with your body. Drape the scarves around your bodies and dance, imagining you are clouds, birds, ballerinas, leaves, etc. Use your imagination and enjoy your exercise together.

Learn to Climb

Make a big pile of couch cushions and large pillows on the floor and let baby climb around in them. As baby improves his climbing skills, set up the cushions in a stair-like way. Once baby is about 9 months old, teach him how to climb real stairs. To do this, put a toy one stair up, and help him move his arms and legs up to get it. To go down, put the toy on the lower step and show him how to go down feet first. No matter how good baby gets at climbing practice, keep stairs blocked off until baby is two years old.

Wit & Wisdom: Make knee pads out of old socks to protect baby's knees when crawling and to put over clothes so they won't get worn out or dirty. Simply cut the toes off and slide them on. If you want extra padding, use a few socks.

—*Cynthia M., Little Rock, AR*

Mirror Dance

Begin the dance by facing each other. The best way to teach baby how to mirror someone is to mirror what baby does, copying his or her movements. Whatever movement baby makes, you do the same thing at the same time. Raise your arms, touch your nose, mess up your hair, or do whatever you think baby is capable of doing back. The older baby is the more dance-like the interaction will become.

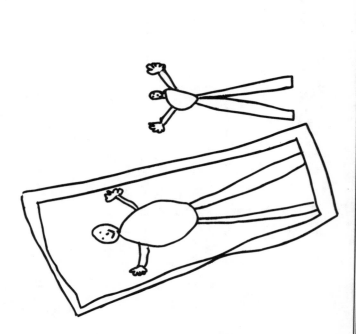

Shake Dance

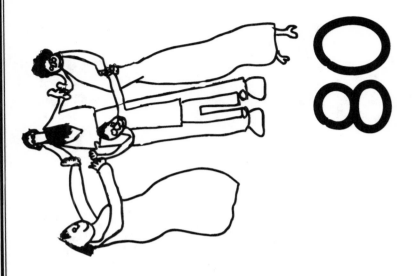

80

Materials
Fast and slow music

All babies like to wiggle, and they like to see their parent wiggling and giggling. Put the music on and starting with your fingertips, arms, and shoulders, begin to shake and wiggle. Then go to the toes and up the legs. Try the head, stomach, and bottom. Wiggle separate body areas or wiggle the whole body. Let baby pick what parts they want to shake and you follow their directions. Wiggle your hands on each other's backs or arms. Make sure to laugh and fall down from exhaustion at the end!

Go Get It

Whether your baby walks, crawls, or runs, they will like this game that will give them lots of exercise and fun. Throw a ball or toy for them to go and get. Have them bring it back to you or to a bucket as quickly as they can. There are all sorts of variations on this. You can throw many things at once and tell them the order in which they have to pick them up. You can throw two colored balls and ask them to get the red one. The main idea is for them to run or crawl around having fun. If they like to throw, let them throw and you retrieve. That way you both get exercise!

Materials
Balls of all sizes
Stuffed animals

Rope Shapes

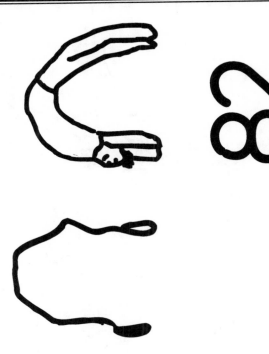

Materials
Rope of any kind

With a jump rope or length of cord, make a simple shape on the floor. Together you and your child try to duplicate the shape with your bodies. Good shapes to try are rectangles, circles, straight lines, triangles, and curved or jagged lines. If other family members or other children are present, you may be able to do more complicated shapes—that is if your floor is large enough!

My Little Locomotor

Materials

Backyard/living room	Favorite toy/ball
Colorful sheet or parachute	Jump rope
Several cushions	Cardboard box
Laundry basket	Mattress

Drape the sheet over a table or chairs to make a tent. Use remaining items to design an obstacle course. You lead the way using the various forms of locomotion your baby has been working so hard to master. Begin with walking or crawling forward, then backward. Also practice squatting and turning. Perhaps your child likes to jump, walk on tiptoe, or roll. You can use the rope as a straight line to direct baby where they should walk next.

Music

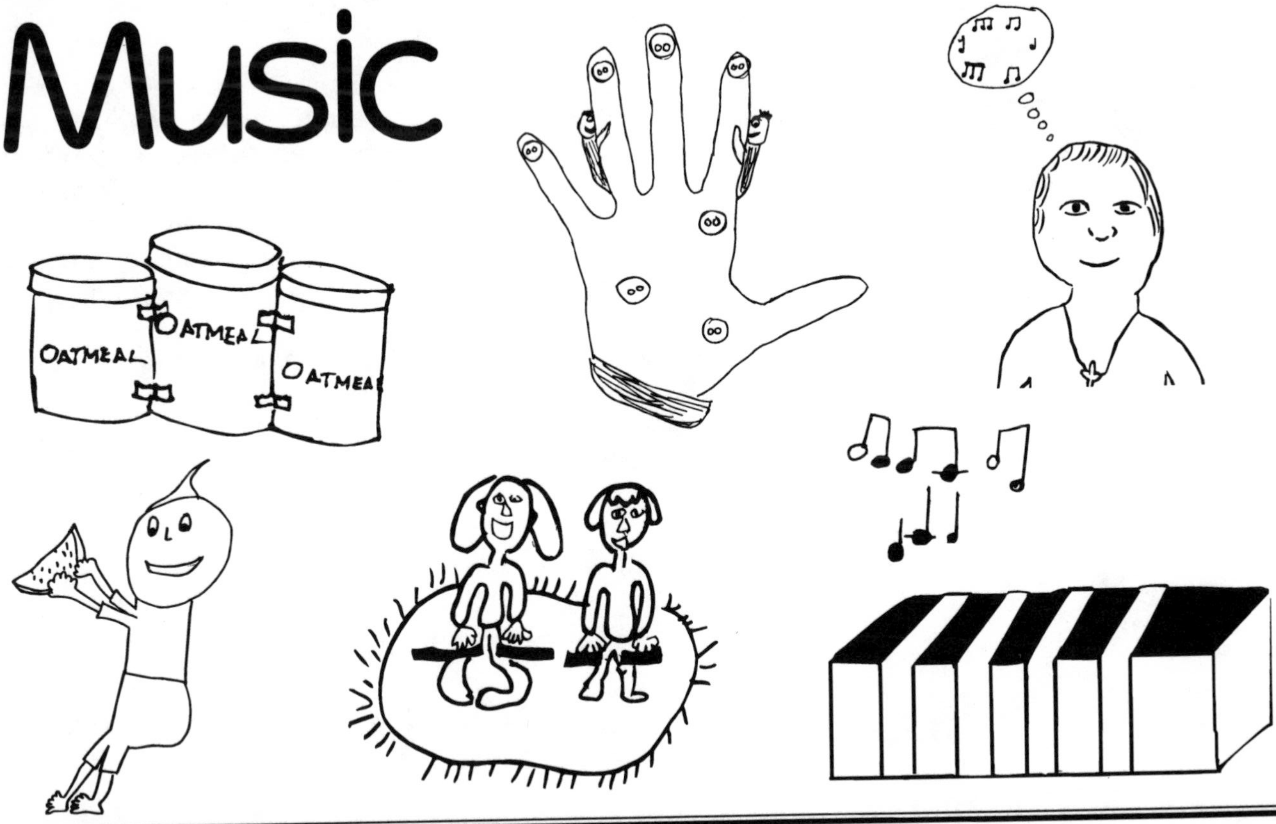

Song with Baby's Name

84

Write a song describing some things baby does each day. You may want to write a wake-up song, a naptime song, a changing or eating song, and a bedtime lullaby. They might go something like this:

Wesley likes to take a bath, take a bath, take a bath
Wesley likes to take a bath early every evening.
Wesley likes to splash around, splash around, splash around
Wesley likes to splash around as Mommy sponges water.

Pick any familiar melody or make one up. Most importantly, when baby hears his own name repeated over and over he feels he is in a safe, familiar place. Every time you do the activity, sing the song. This may even help baby identify and form patterns of behavior. For instance, if the same song is sung before naptime every day, just hearing the song might make baby tired. Now that is worth a try!

Self-Made Songs

85

Listen to baby babble. Sometimes there is a rhythm to the words or sounds. Baby may repeat the same sound melodically over and over. Once a pattern is detected, hum along or say the words baby is saying. Even singing la, la, la to baby's gurgling is song-like. Any sound baby makes is active communication. Take advantage of baby's efforts by joining in. Baby will be delighted and feel important at the same time.

Shake and Rattle

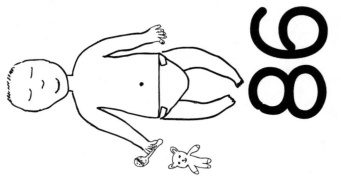

86

Materials
Old plastic film canisters
Music-making objects: dry beans, marbles, rice, pop-
corn, bells, pebbles

Put the objects into the film containers. Objects may
be put with same objects or mixed up, depending on
how many film containers are available. Put a container in each of baby's hands and, holding them, shake
the containers. Try humming a tune or singing a song
as baby shakes. You could also do a dance as baby
laughs. Don't forget to bring these on trips for quick
entertainment.

Note: This must be closely supervised since it
involves small things that baby could choke on.

your Child's Voice

Materials
Tape recorder
Cassette tape

Put a cassette tape in the tape recorder and give a little spoken introduction about your baby: age, date, things baby likes to do, baby's favorite foods, personality traits, etc. Record your child's voice, laughing, crying, babbling, and breathing. Sing songs, clap hands, and do whatever you do together each day. Plan on adding to this tape periodically so that baby can hear the music of his or her own voice over time.

87

MUSIC MAKER

Foot and Hand Jingles

Materials
1/4" elastic
Bells of any kind

Cut elastic to fit around baby's wrists and ankles, making sure not to make it too tight. Sew the ends of the elastic together making a bracelet shape, then sew the bells onto the elastic. How many bells you sew on will determine how much noise baby makes. Put the bracelets around baby's wrists and ankles. Put some music on and help baby shake her hands and feet to the music. Laugh, sing along, and make faces. You may even want to get a pan, spoon, or lid and participate in the music! Hold baby in your arms and dance around to the music, shaking the bells as you twirl!

88

Guess the Noise

Here's a game that can be played anywhere. It will teach baby to listen carefully and become more sensitive to sounds. Baby shuts his eyes and guesses the sounds you are making. Here are a few ideas:

Kitchen: Water dripping, fork on the sink, fork on a glass or pan, putting a lid on a pan, refrigerator door opening, microwave bell, etc.

Around the House: Ball bouncing on the floor, phone dialing or ringing, door closing, etc. When baby's old enough, you can take turns making the sounds and guessing.

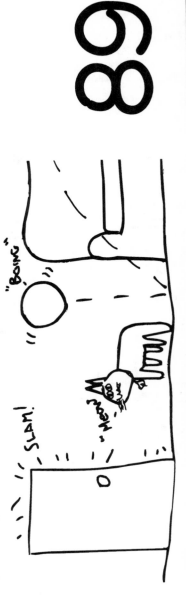

89

Music Is Hiding

Materials
Musical toy baby likes

Wind up the musical toy baby likes and hide it somewhere in the room. Ask baby, "Where is the music?" Crawl around the room together looking for the music. If baby is old enough, have him hide the toy while you shut your eyes, and then look for the toy. Baby will be full of giggles if he hides the toy and you make a big deal of finding it—but not right away of course!

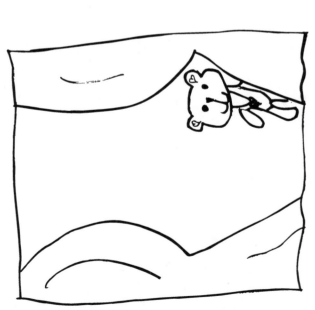

Rhythm Sticks

Materials

Lengths of wood dowelling 6 to 8 inches long by 1/2 to 1 inch diameter (most lumber stores will cut the dowelling to your specifications)

Sandpaper

High-gloss acrylic paint

Sand the ends of the dowels until smooth. Paint the rhythm sticks in a variety of bright colors. Let them dry completely before using. Dowels can also be left a natural wood color by staining them. Make sure that anything put on the dowels is non-toxic. There are many games to play with rhythm sticks. Below are a few, starting at 3 months old.

- Hum a melody while you tap the sticks together lightly.
- As baby begins to hold things, let him hold one in each hand as you hold one in each hand. Do a made up patty cake type tapping.
- As baby begins to crawl, put the rhythm sticks on the floor and let baby push them as she crawls.
- Put on a music tape and tap together.
- Get siblings in on it by letting them make up a special stick dance for baby to watch.

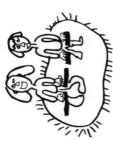

Song of Humor

Singing is a good way for baby to start developing a sense of humor. Silly, ridiculous verses bring out giggles in baby even at one year old. Find some songs or make up one of your own. Start with everyday things like brushing teeth, and make them silly:

"This is the way we brush our toes. . . ."
"Twinkle, Twinkle, little donut . . . ."
"Mary had a little whale . . . ."
"I know an old lady who swallowed a cow . . . ."

At the very least you might laugh, and baby might think, which promotes mental growth in both of you.

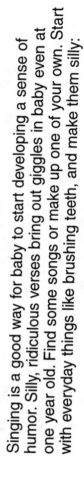

Rubber Band Harp

93

Materials
Several rubber bands of many sizes and
thicknesses
Shoebox

Stretch the rubber bands across the shoebox. Pluck the bands with your fingers and
you and baby can listen to the different
sounds. Try holding the rubber band in the
middle and plucking. What happens to the
sound? Also, try strumming the fingers
across all of the bands. Baby will have fun
pulling and letting go, as long as the
bands are not so close together that he
gets his fingers pinched.

Bongo Drums

Materials
3 different size oatmeal cylinders
Masking tape

Tape the cylinders together to make a set of drums. Set the drums on baby's lap or between the two of you on the floor. Briefly demonstrate how to beat each drum with your fingers, palms, knuckles, and heels of the hand. Put some music on and tap to the beat.

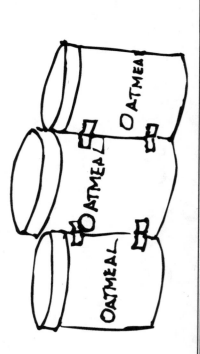

Louder, Softer Please

Sing a familiar song, such as "Yankee Doodle." Start singing it loudly, gradually singing more softly as if Yankee Doodle were riding off into the distance. Sing more of the song, this time getting louder and louder as if Yankee were riding toward you. This little exercise helps your child understand the dynamics of sound and music. Both of you can sing songs together, changing the volume to suit the words and meaning of the songs.

Finger Tapping

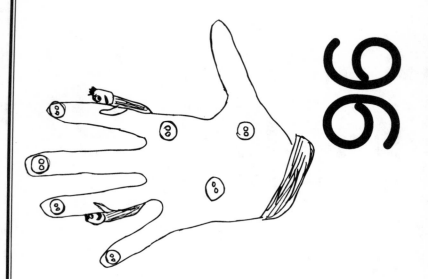

Materials
Old pair of children's gloves
10 buttons
Needle and thread

Sew the buttons onto the fingertips of each glove. Put the gloves on baby and begin tapping with the fingertips on a table or a non-carpeted floor. Experiment with other surfaces: stone, metal, bone, marble, plastic, formica, or ceramic. Listen to the different sounds that each surface produces. Baby may want to keep the gloves on as he crawls around making a clicking sound.

Story Sound Effects

Make up or read a familiar story to your child. The story should involve many sound effects, animals, and silly characters. As you tell the story, sing some of the words and have your child make all the sound effects. Add fun hand and body movements if baby likes it.

Everyday Toys

Black and White Pictures

Materials
White paper
Black markers

Newborn babies are attracted to the sharply contrasting colors of black and white. They also like the bold patterns of diagonals, bulls-eyes, and checkerboards. The human face is a favorite of all babies. Take the white paper and make a simple face with hair, eyebrows, eyes, nose, and mouth. Make some other patterns. Tape your masterpieces to the inside of the crib, the bassinet, or the car window. Babies see best seven to nine inches from their face.

Mobiles

Materials

Embroidery hoop, hanger, or pie tin
Heavyweight string or yarn
Assorted household objects
  or small stuffed animals
Ceiling hook

The idea of a mobile is to hang household objects from the hanger, pie tin, or embroidery hoop. The mobile is then hung from the ceiling by a hook. Here are a few ideas to get you started:

1. Light mobile: take pieces of cardboard, cut into different shapes, and cover them with securely fastened aluminum foil. When light from a window hits the foil, it will reflect around the room.

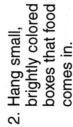

2. Hang small, brightly colored boxes that food comes in.

3. Hang small stuffed animals or figures face down so baby can look up and see them.

4. Hang small jingle bells or other things that make a musical sound when a breeze hits them.

When baby is old enough to reach up and touch or pull on the hanging objects, make sure that the mobile and its objects are tied securely.

Textured Touch

Materials
Assorted textured pieces: velvet, silk, terry cloth, burlap, leather, fake fur, corduroy, sandpaper

Flat box with lid (tie or scarf boxes work well)

Take the thin box and punch two finger holes in the top next to each other. Put a textured piece in the box. Show baby how to put a finger in the box and feel the texture, then put your finger in the box and play with baby's finger as you both feel the textured piece. Talk about the object and texture you are feeling: smooth, rough, silky, fuzzy, etc.

Wit & Wisdom: Take an old rubber suction soap dish and give it to baby for teething. Also, the suction cups can be put on things within baby's reach, such as the refrigerator. They will love to pull it off and hear the suction pop.

—Jan Collins, Edina, MN

100

Pictures to Chew

Materials
Plastic photo album pages, plastic protector sheets, or laminator
Colored magazine pictures
Glue
Colored paper

Cut pictures so that two are the same size, then glue them back to back. Pictures can also be glued to a piece of colored paper. Slip the pictures inside the plastic cover and glue the edges shut. Baby can look at the pictures and chew on the edges without ruining a good book. You may want to put the pages together by punching holes in the side and tying the pages together with yarn or string. If plastic covers seem like too much work, simply prepare pic- tures by gluing them back to back, then take the pictures to a copy store and have them laminated. To save money, have them laminate the pictures onto one big sheet and do the cutting yourself, as the copy stores charge per cut.

Wit & Wisdom: A soft, clean toothbrush makes a great teething toy, massaging gums at the same time.

—*Chris N., San Antonio, TX*

101

Discovery Rattle

Materials

Small noisemakers that are interesting to look at, like colored buttons, shiny beads or sequins, bells, or beans

Contact cement or hot glue gun

Cloth tape

Small, clear plastic storage box with many compartments, yet small enough for baby to hold

Place noisemakers into separate compartments in the storage box. Glue the cover shut, and after the glue is dry, seal the seam with cloth tape.

Note: Two other ideas to try: 1) Make a quiet box with things like feathers, glitter, or ripped paper so baby can watch items float around in the container. Make sure to use a container that will allow some space for the floating. 2) Make a viewing box with items that baby shouldn't touch, but would love to look at, like fishing tackle or holiday ornaments.

Floor Roller

Materials
2 clear, empty two-liter beverage containers
Small toys and balls
Epoxy cement or glue gun
Plastic or cloth tape

Cut the top off of the beverage containers one-third of the way down. Put the toys in one of the container halves. Wedge one beverage container over the other, closing the unit, and forming one oblong container. Glue container closed and, once dry, tape the seams. Put the container on the floor and show baby how to crawl along, pushing it as you go. It is fun to watch everything inside roll around. Baby may also like to pick up the container and drop it, or watch the toys fall from one end and to the other.

Personal Picture Book

104

Materials

Photo albums with self-adhesive pages
Photos of family, friends, pets, food, nature, toys, clothes, etc.

Make up a few books of your own for baby to look at. Since baby doesn't read, simply tell a different story each time you look at the pictures together. Use people and objects that baby can see every day. Talk about and describe what the people are doing. Talk about the way things function in their daily use. You may even walk to the object or person in the house, hold up the picture, and say, "same." Put only one picture per page so baby is not confused with what you are talking about. Use magazines, greeting cards, and catalogues as well as your own photos. It is also fun to make a book using only pictures of baby.

Finger Puppets

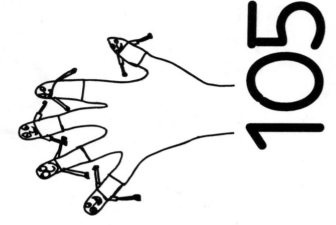

Materials
Old gloves
Colored felt pieces
Paint pens
Needle and thread

Cut the fingers off the glove and sew the fingers' cut edges under 1/2 inch to prevent unraveling. Cut the felt pieces to make ears, nose, hat, whiskers, arms, etc. Using fabric pens, make faces and add detail. Make up stories about the puppets and give them names. Play hide and seek, making the puppets disappear under a pillow or behind a doll. When baby gets bored, wiggle them around close to baby while making funny sounds!

Clothespin Fun

Materials

Large container that has smooth edges when the lid is removed

Clothespins: the kind that you don't have to pinch to open

Here are four fun games you and baby can play with your clothespins and container:

1. Stand above the container and drop the clothespins in, or stand two to three feet away and try to toss the clothespins in.
2. Sit on the floor next to the container and slip the clothespins around the top. Then take them off and put them on again.
3. Put the clothespins inside the container, then put the plastic lid back on and place the container on the floor and roll it around.
4. Turn the container over and use the clothespins like drumsticks.

Stringing Box

Materials
Large wooden beads
Large macaroni tubes
Colored shoelaces with plastic tips
Shoebox

This activity should not be done until baby is out of the "put everything in mouth" stage, unless the beads are very large. Put all the supplies in a shoebox and decorate it if you like. Tie a large bead to the end of the shoelace so that all the beads don't fall off as you begin to string. First, simply help baby to string randomly; later, make simple patterns that baby can copy, like red, blue, red, or two beads, one macaroni. Tie the shoe strings together when you are finished to make a necklace or hanging decoration.

Golf Tee Hammer Box

Materials
Strong, small box
Jumbo golf tees
Wooden play hammer

Turn the box upside down. First, hammer the jumbo golf tees into the box to make the holes, then pull the tees up and let baby hammer away! Soon baby will get the hang of it and start pulling the tees up just to hammer them down again. Happy hammering!

108

Bead Catcher

Materials
Plastic scooper from a large box of detergent
String or ribbon 8 inches long
1 inch bead
1/2 inch bead

Poke a hole in the bottom of the plastic scoop. Thread the string or ribbon through the hole in the scoop. Tie the 1/2 inch bead to one end of the string so it can't slip back through the hole. Tie the one inch bead to the other end of the string. Show the child how to swing the bead up and around in the air to catch it in the scooper. Make one for yourself as well so you can play together. If your child is not coordinated enough to catch the bead in the cup, set up small plastic figures or blocks. Then, holding the scoop above them, swing the bead to knock them over.

109

Paper Balls

Materials
Newspaper
Masking tape
Cardboard box

Scrunch newspaper into small, medium, and large balls. Wrap masking tape around the outside of the newspaper ball to hold the crunched edges together. Roll the ball on the floor, trying to knock something over, or throw it into the box. Play catch or kick the ball. Baby may come up with a game or two of their own. The good news is that paper ball games can be played inside!

Kitchen Boxes

Materials
Collect small boxes that food comes in—the smaller and brighter the better

Make sure the box is clean, then stuff it with wadded-up newspaper to help it keep its shape. Tape it shut with thick tape that won't peel off. When baby is very little, they may chew on the boxes or stack them up like blocks, but as soon as they start watching you work in the kitchen, they will want to copy you! Set up a mini-kitchen for them using larger cardboard boxes or an old hutch. Whenever you are tempted to throw away measuring cups, spoons, pans, etc., donate them to baby's kitchen. Garage sales are a great place to find make-believe toys. Go together on a Saturday to search for pans, aprons, tea sets, etc.

111

Floor Time

Magic Mirror

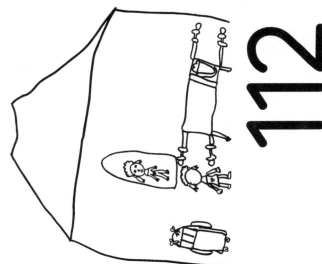

112

Materials
Non-breakable mirror
Scarf

Gaze into the mirror with baby to make faces together. Begin with no expression, and slowly change to a smiling one. Use short, descriptive phrases such as, "I look happy," "I feel silly," "see my mouth." Now, slowly change to a sad expression and say, "I look sad." Drape the scarf over the mirror and play peek-a-boo with your reflections. Say, "I see (baby's name)." Baby will gradually discover whose reflections are in the mirror and the "magic" that makes them move.

Welcome to My World

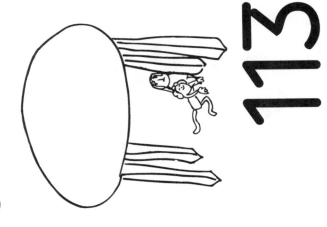

Explore your baby's world from their per-spective: see what they see, touch what they touch, smell what they smell, hear what they hear. Pretend you're a baby too! What does that table look like underneath? How about the ceiling? Wow, is everything huge or what?

Wit & Wisdom: Take pictures of your child's favorite stuffed animals with the animals' names written in front of them. It will help your child remember their special friends when they grow up.

—*Ana Marie P., Salt Lake City, UT*

113

Box of Socks

114

Materials
Laundry basket or box
Socks of different sizes

A good use for all those unmatched socks is to let baby have fun trying them on and pulling them off. Try to choose loose fitting socks—you know, the kind that don't require a crowbar to remove! When baby tires of trying the socks on, they may want to throw them in the air and watch them float to the floor. The basket or box is also fun to explore.

Wit & Wisdom: If you have two siblings close in age, find some way to let them do things individually. It will cut down on sibling squabbles.

—*Trisha R., Boston, MA*

Fill and Roll

Materials
Clean oatmeal container with lid
Tennis balls, favorite stuffed animal, toy cars, or any object baby has fun playing with that fits inside the oatmeal container

Put whatever object you want inside the oatmeal container and put the lid on. With baby in front of you, each of you roll the container on the floor back and forth to each other. Say "what's inside?" and encourage baby to take the top off and empty the container. Of course, many babies need no encouragement and will peel the top off, empty the contents, and squeal with joy before you can blink!

Crawl Space Race

Crawl together in a hallway or open area to capture a favorite object or see a favorite person. This game becomes more elaborate as baby grows. You can play stop and go, hide and seek, and the classic family favorite, "last one in the bathtub is a silly pie," a "wet noodle," or a "rotten egg," ...you get the idea. This kind of fun is bound to make you laugh, and baby loves that sound!

Wit & Wisdom: Don't be afraid when baby has a fever. The temperature means the body is fighting. Of course, if the temperature is too high, call the doctor.

—Kathleen Horst, St. Paul, MN

116

Cheerio!

When you first notice baby's interest in pouring, let her go for it. With cereal (like Cheerios), provide paper cups, empty egg cartons, or any other container into which they can pour. Babies love this work. Watch how they pinch and scoop the cereal into their cups. Of course, they will probably eat half the Cheerios, but that's half the fun!

Wit & Wisdom: When I took my baby out to eat in restaurants, I always carried her baby spoon in a toothbrush container in my purse.

—Carrie P., Napa, CA

117

Magic Act

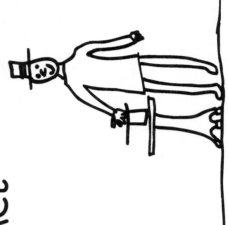

Materials
Empty rectangular Kleenex tissue box
Colorful scarves or similar material

Tie the scarves together end to end and put them into the Kleenex box with a small piece peeking out. Because of baby's curious nature and busy hands, they will enjoy pulling the long scarf out of its hiding place. If they don't pull the scarf out by themselves, show them how. Pull gently and say, "I'm pulling the scarf, now you pull." Baby will most likely want to pull the scarves out a few times in a row before moving on to something else. Once the scarves are out of the box, wiggle them on the floor like a snake. Baby may also like holding the scarf while crawling around the house.

118

Wrap It Up!

Materials
Favorite baby toys: cars, blocks, Wiffle ball, cup, spoon, stuffed animal, etc.
Tissue paper or old wrapping paper
Tape

Wrap toys like presents in the tissue paper and place them near baby. Say, "I think these are yours." Each bundle is fun for baby to unwrap, even though the objects inside are familiar favorites. Have plenty of tape ready. As you've probably learned by now, if something is fun for baby once, it is just as fun the second time.

Wit & Wisdom: I put my son's artwork in a three-ring binder, starting with his first scribble. His portfolio is now in its third volume and he looks at it often.
—*Julia York, Walnut Creek, CA*

119

Bouncing Cupcakes

Materials
Cupcake pan
3 to 6 tennis balls
Pillowcase or paper shopping bag

Place cupcake pan and balls into the pillow-case. Sit with baby on the floor. Show baby the pillowcase and say, "let's look inside" or "what's inside this bag?" Baby has several tasks to choose from: tipping the pillowcase to spill contents out, reaching inside to pull contents out, bouncing the balls, putting the balls into the cupcake pan, taking the balls out of the pan, tipping the pan over to hide balls underneath. Leave it to baby to invent new uses for every-day objects!

My Beautiful Balloon

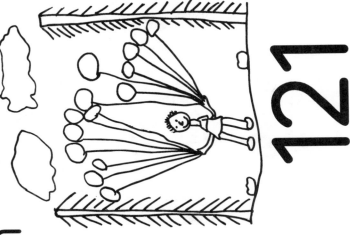

Materials
Balloons
String

Babies love balloons. They're colorful, lightweight, and magical. They seem to float and fly, which is what most babies believe they can do as well. Whether baby is crawling or walking, pulling something on a string is a grand lesson in cause and effect. Baby moves and the balloon moves along too. You take a turn at pulling the balloon and ask baby to follow it. Remind baby to be gentle with the balloon. Baby will also love to throw balloons in the air, watch them fall to the ground, and kick them around the room. They may even try sitting on them to pop them. **Be extremely careful to pick up all pieces of any popped balloons, as they are a major cause of choking in babies.**

121

Stack Attack

Materials
Wooden blocks (unit blocks, all sizes and shapes)

Begin to collect blocks now because their value is immeasurable and they will be used for years to come. They are fun to hold, carry, drop, stack, knock over, pull, push, and sort. With experience, baby will construct rows, simple bridges, enclosures, and patterns. Eventually blocks are transformed into food, animals, vehicles, boats, trains, planes, walls, roads, rivers, train tracks, buildings, furniture, tools, and mountains in baby's imagination. Store blocks in a basket or plastic container where baby is able to reach them. Low, sturdy shelves are ideal for holding blocks and other favorite toys. As you explore blocks together, observe baby's choices. Use descriptive words, such as smooth, hard, curved, pointed, and straight. Blocks never lose their value, and never go out of style.

122

Make Me a Match

Materials
Masking tape
Laundry basket or box
Things in sets of two: coasters, paper napkins, gloves, large earrings, socks, spoons, shoes, etc.

Create a trail with masking tape on the floor. Use as much floor space as possible. Place one item from each matching set along the trail, and keep the other matching item in the basket at the beginning of the trail. Ask baby to choose one thing from the basket and say, "let's find something that looks just like this. I will follow you." (A push-cart, lightweight wagon, or box is fun for baby to drop items into as matches are found.) Do one match, setting it at the end of your trail. Go back to the beginning and do another match. Make a large square shape on the floor with masking tape at the end of the trail to put the found matches in.

123

Twisting and Turning

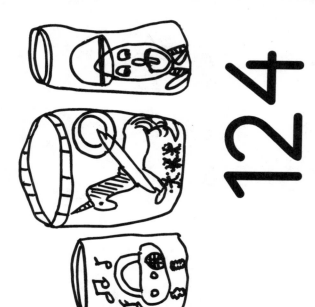

Materials
Several plastic jars with lids that twist off
(Small baby food jars are good if played
with on carpeted area)

Place a small figure, plastic animal, large
beads, or buttons into the jars. Close the lids
loosely. Sit with baby on floor and say, "I
need help opening these jars, how do we
open these?" Questions like these encourage problem-solving. You support baby's
efforts by being near and providing uninterrupted time for baby to find a solution. In
other words, don't just jump in and open the
jar after baby has tried for 30 seconds!
Praise baby's efforts, even if the results
aren't what you expected.

124

Tub of Delights

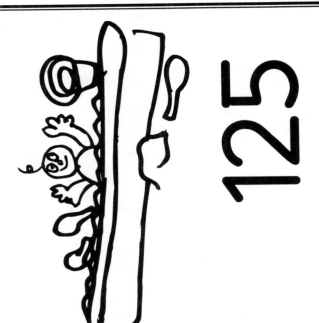

Materials

Large plastic tub with cover or shallow
   cardboard box with cover
Set of plastic or metal measuring cups
Funnel, strainer, ice cream scoop
One of the following: dried beans, rice, sand,
   cornmeal, birdseed, dried pasta shapes

Pour one of the dried goods into the container.
Sit on the floor or stand around a child-size
table with baby and play in the tub. Use words
to describe what you feel, for example, "This
rice feels hard." As you fill, pour, and stir, continue to give baby words for what is happening.
It is fun to hide small plastic toys in the dried
goods, so as baby digs around, surprises are
found. Touch, like all baby's senses, gives baby
valuable information about the world.

125

Tube Slide

Materials
Different sizes of cardboard tube, the
longer the better
Small cars or balls
Large narrow box (optional)

Balance one end of the tube on a couch, stool,
or pillow. Put the other end of the tube on the
ground so that the tube is angled downward like
a slide. Put balls, cars, etc., in the tube at the
top and watch them come out at the bottom.
Babies will do this for long periods of time,
always amazed that the object comes out at the
other end! If you want a more permanent struc-
ture, cut holes through the box and push the
tubes through at various angles.

Soft Ball Socks

Materials
Bucket or laundry basket
Socks

Roll the socks inside themselves to form soft balls. You may want to put one strip of masking tape around the ball to help it stay in a ball shape. Start tossing the socks into the basket. Begin close to the basket and back up as baby gets better at making baskets. You can make a variety of games out of soft ball socks. Set up some plastic figures and roll the socks toward them on the floor, or throw the ball trying to hit them. Play catch with the socks. Throw them up in the air and catch them. Feel free to make up your own games while you and baby play.

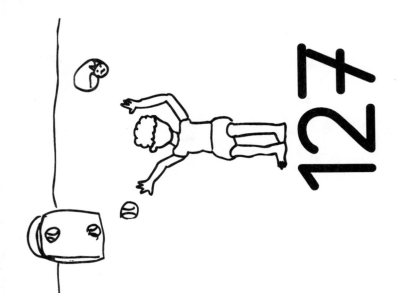

See Saw

Materials
Book
Paper tube
Newspaper
Small toys or stuffed animals

Take the tube and stuff it full of newspapers. Lay the tube horizontally on the floor. Put the book on top of the tube, balanced in the middle like a see saw. Collect a basket of small toys and stuffed animals and put one at a time on the down side of the see saw. Push the up side of the see saw down, and watch the toy fly in the air. After all animals have had a chance to fly, pick them up and start again.

Wit & Wisdom: Carry a plastic spray bottle of water in your diaper bag so if baby drops a pacifier, teething ring, or bottle you can spray it off.

—David E., Houston, TX

128

Art

BROWN

RED

BROWN

RED

The Art's in the Doing

What "art" can baby make? Well, to begin with, you and baby will create together. Then as baby grows, is able to hold a marker or paintbrush, and learns through experience that not everything is edible, art experiences change. Some things that do not change are: you must supply the appropriate supplies, model the use of various tools, closely supervise, facilitate baby's exploration, and clean up. Always remember that the process is more important than the final product! Take a few minutes and remember some of your earliest art experiences. What materials did you use? Do you remember how you felt? What was your favorite form of expression? As you approach each new art experience with baby, enjoy yourself, and allow baby to show you what "artistic freedom" really means.

Wit & Wisdom: I found a great way to save my son's drawings. I simply glue them onto an old calendar.

—Ian P., Sedona, AZ

Contact Collage

Materials
1 roll of clear contact paper
Magazine pictures of children, animals, toys, nature, etc.
Small pieces of fabric: felt, burlap, velvet, corduroy, or denim
Scissors
Tape

Cut a large piece of contact paper and tape it to the floor or at baby's eye level on the wall with the backing facing up. Then peel off the backing (peel around the tape). Cut pictures from magazines and a variety of fabric shapes. Pick a picture or piece of material and place it on the sticky contact paper. Let baby choose which pieces, and observe and talk about her choices using descriptive phrases such as, "You chose a picture of a red ball."

Crumple Crazy

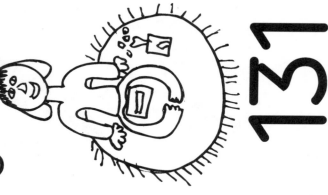

131

Materials
White tissue paper (other colors are great, but dyes will transfer onto hands when tissue is wet)
Cardboard: cereal box, poster board, or construction paper
Glue

Mix one teaspoon water and two tablespoons glue in a small container. Cut or tear tissue paper into small pieces. Crumple tissue paper. Squeeze or brush some glue onto the cardboard and "hide" the glue with crumpled tissue paper. Baby may decide to simply tear and crumple. Then again, baby might want to squeeze or pour glue onto the cardboard until it resembles a small puddle. If you're not up for this experience, use a glue stick. Remember, babies learn what's too much by using too much.

Fingers, Hands, and Elbows Too

Materials
Liquid tempera paint (any color)
Plastic tray, cookie sheet, or lid of rectangular tub
Several sheets of heavyweight drawing paper or finger painting paper
Dish of warm, soapy water
Towel

Pour three tablespoons of paint into the tray. Dip and move your fingers around in the paint. Describe how the paint feels on your hands. Encourage baby to feel the paint. You feel it too—it might bring back early memories! Use your index finger to draw something baby might recognize. Let baby draw shapes. Another surface to use is a large glass window, which allows baby endless space to create. Simply hose the window off when done. Before washing up, place your hands in the paint, then onto a nearby sheet of paper. This is a fun way to use that paint, and make handprints at the same time.

Wit & Wisdom: I let my daughter finger paint right on her highchair tray. It was easy to clean up and she was secure in one place. She especially liked painting with colored pudding. She would suck her thumb and get a pleasant surprise!

—*Anna S., Seattle, WA*

Musical Chalk

Materials
Sidewalk chalk
Masking tape
Large pieces of paper
Liquid starch
Small paintbrush

Play music you love while baby makes his chalk dance on paper. Wrap one end of the chalk with masking tape. This cuts down on the amount of chalk on baby's hands. Tape paper to a work surface: refrigerator, child-size table, or floor. Play music. Say, "listen to the music" and "let's make our chalk dance on the paper." Work with dry chalk on dry paper initially. Once baby has some chalk experience, use dry chalk and paper brushed with a light coat of liquid starch.

Another method is to leave the paper dry and dip the chalk into a small container of starch. The chalk must be dipped several times with this last technique. The larger the paper the better, since it gives baby freedom to use whole arm movements, which is exactly what baby needs.

133

Sandpaper Line Designs

Materials
Coarse sandpaper
Yarn of any kind

Cut the yarn into several different lengths, using as much or as little as you want. Different textures and colors will make the picture more interesting. Pick up the yarn and put a piece on the sandpaper, showing baby how it's done. The yarn will stick to the sandpaper as you and baby create designs together. If you want to change your designs, go ahead—simply move the yarn. Put these reusable materials in a zip-lock bag. Wherever you are, this is a quiet, clean art experience.

Wit & Wisdom:

> I see, and I remember,
> I do, and I understand.
>
> —*Chinese Proverb*

134

A Box Is a Box

Materials
Any size box with staples removed
Liquid tempera paint
Paintbrush or small sponge paint roller
Newspapers or drop cloth

A box is a box until baby paints it. Then it's a beautiful craft and imaginative toy! If you can suspend disbelief, your box transforms many times over: into a garage, mailbox, cave, house, railroad station, castle, boat, and yes, even a hat. Spread the drop cloth or newspapers on the ground to make clean-up easier, and to define the workspace. Put 1/4 cup paint in a sturdy plastic container or tray. Put the box on the newspaper and set the paintbrush close. See what baby does with the brush before you put it into the paint. You may decide to use two brushes so that you can paint at the same time as baby. Hold the paint container so it won't spill as baby haphazardly dips the brush. Expect a little mess, and dress accordingly.

The Scribble

Materials
Large paper (experiment with different types)
Large non-toxic watercolor markers
Large crayons

When baby draws and scribbles, something that never existed is created. What joy there is in being able to express thoughts and feelings in this way, not to mention the pure pleasure of using the materials! Put the paper on the floor or a low table that has been covered with newspaper. It also works to tape the paper to the refrigerator front at baby's eye level. Place the markers or crayons in a tray next to the paper. Make sure to say, "the markers are for drawing on the paper." Sit and draw with baby. Save some drawings each month and make a book for baby's birthday each year. This is a great way to "see" creativity grow and develop.

Wit & Wisdom: Remove crayon marks from wallpaper with a hairdryer set on hot. First, the wax heats up, then it can be wiped off with a damp cloth and oil soap.

—*Jared Sellers, Foster City, CA*

136

Moving Masterpiece

Materials

Tempera paint

Pie tin or clean styrofoam meat/vegetable tray

Large pieces of paper: butcher paper, newsprint, the backside of unused wallpaper, wrapping paper

Ball: tennis ball, golf ball, baseball (lightweight plastic balls will not roll with paint on them)

Choose an area that's easy to clean up, like the floor, patio, garage, or deck. Spread newspapers on the work surface and place the paper on top. Set the ball in the paint and roll it around a little before setting it on the paper to roll to baby. Say, "Roll the ball" and "Roll the ball on the paper." Your adventurous child might try bouncing the ball on the paper, so beware. It's also fun to dip the wheels of a favorite plastic or wooden vehicle in the paint and zoom it across the paper.

137

Shapes

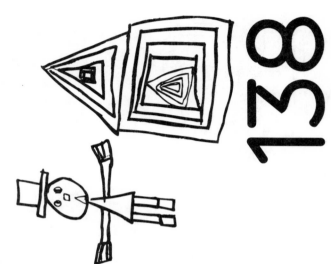

Materials
Flat sponges
Washable liquid paint
Paper
3 flat pans or plates to put paint in

Cut sponge into one geometric shape of different sizes. For example, do squares and make a
small, medium, and large square. Pour colored
paints into three flat containers and put a
sponge in each. Help baby to dip the sponge in
the paint and then press it onto the paper. Make
any design you want. Once the paint has dried,
cut the sheet of paper into the geometric shape
you used. Take a walk inside or outside with
baby. While holding up the shaped piece, find
other things that are the same shape.

Potato Prints

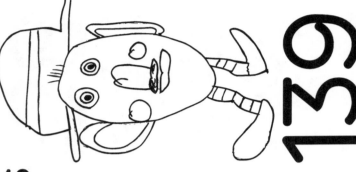

Materials

Potato   Paper
Paint   Sponge
Knife   Paintbrush

Cut the potato in half. Use the knife to cut out a design on the potato. Whatever is raised will be seen on the print. Take a paintbrush and spread some of the paint onto the sponge; that way when baby dips the potato into the paint there won't be a dripping mess! Press the potato print onto the paper. Wash the potato off if another color is used and keep printing!

Wit & Wisdom: It's amazing what you can find around the house to use in paint printing. My granddaughter loves using the following: a toothbrush, berry basket, corks, whisks, cookie cutters, and toilet paper tubes.

—*Sara Shiffman, Playa Del Rey, CA*

139

Foil with Oil

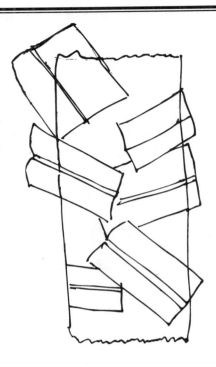

Materials
Baby oil
Tin foil or wax paper
Small pieces of art tissue paper (not
    Kleenex tissue)

Cut or tear tissue paper in small pieces.
Tear off a piece of foil or wax paper as
large as the piece of art will be. Squeeze
a drop or two of oil onto the foil. Place one
of the tissue paper pieces on top. The
paper will stick, but it is not permanent.
Layer tissue paper to create a collage
using different colors for contrast. This is a
great sensory experience for baby, and it
smells nice too.

Color Search

Materials
White paper
Crayons
Paper bag

Take a crayon and draw a blotch of color on the paper. Tell baby what color it is, then go exploring around the house or in baby's room for things that are that color. Put them in the paper bag, or simply point them out if they won't fit in the bag. Sit down and pull each item out of the bag and, as baby plays with the toy, talk about the color again. You may want to talk about the same color for a week so baby can learn to recognize it. Or you may want to do three different colors in one day just for the fun of it.

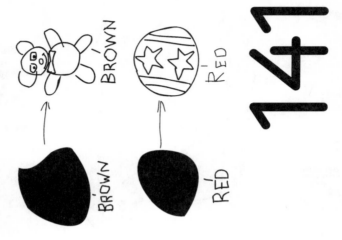

BROWN

BROWN

RED

RED

141

Stained Glass Window

Materials
Assorted colored cellophane
Scissors
Tape

Cut the cellophane into small two to three inch squares or different shapes. Have baby hold the piece of cellophane up to the window as you tape it on. Add many pieces until a large square resembling a stained glass window is made. As light shines through the window, enjoy the color and design with baby.

Blob Painting

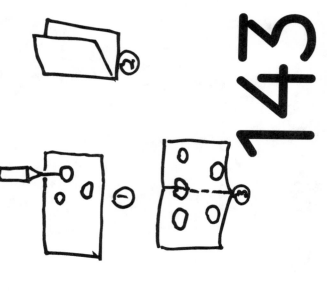

Materials
2 to 3 small plastic cosmetic bottles (the travel kind)
Tempera paint
Paper

Put a different color of paint into each bottle. Baby can squeeze the paint onto the paper in small puddles. Once many small puddles are on the paper, fold the paper in half and rub lightly over the top causing a print to be made. It is also fun to put blobs of paint all over one piece of paper, then put another piece of paper over the top and rub.

143

Watercolor

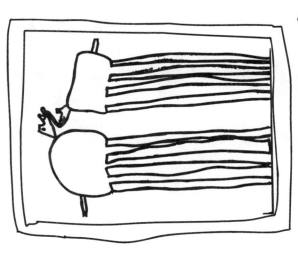

Materials

Watercolor paint (the kind you get at the
grocery store in a plastic case)
Paper
Paintbrush
Crayons

Watercolor is one of the easiest forms of
painting a baby can do. The paint is easier
to get out of clothes and there is less mess
all around. Get a dish full of water and show
baby how to dip the paintbrush into the
water, then the paint. You may want to get a
piece of paper yourself and make some
pretty stationery. It's also fun to do a crayon
drawing first, then paint over the top so the
crayon still shows through.

144

Rubber Stamp Art

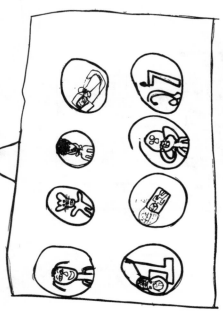

145

Materials
Rubber stamps of any kind
Non-toxic ink pad
Paper

Rubber stamps are so fun for baby to use
and make great pictures or designs.
Simply put the piece of paper on the table,
press the rubber stamp into the ink pad,
and stamp onto the paper. Show baby a
few times first, then let her have a turn.

Nature

Meet the Animals

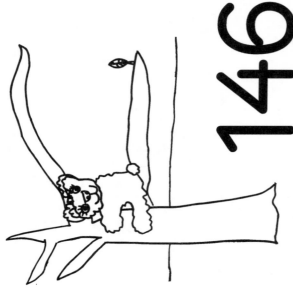

Even young babies are enchanted when in the presence of animals. Something about the color, sound, and movement puts them into a trance. If you don't have any animals of your own, consider a zoo or farm trip. Most zoos have a petting area where baby can feed goats, lambs, horses, and sometimes a pig or two. Before you go to visit animals, look at picture books or watch a video tape about them. While at the zoo or farm, don't just stroll past, instead, sit and watch your favorite animals for a little while, as it's the only way to get to know a particular animal's behavior.

Special Tree

Materials
Buy a seedling tree
Small shovel

Find a place to plant your tree: in your yard, at a local park, or at a nearby school. On baby's birthday or any special day you choose, go with baby to plant the tree. Once the tree is planted, go back often to water and care for it. Tell baby the tree belongs to him or her and do the following things together: watch the tree grow and change, measure baby and measure the tree, name the tree, care for the tree, and most of all, play, sing, and laugh around baby's special tree.

Wit & Wisdom: A young tree is a great gift to send a parent or grandparent when a new baby is born. This is a constant reminder to the receiver of their very special child.
—*Shirley Crescini, Lockford, CA*

147

Sky's the Limit

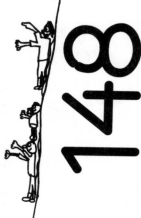

148

Materials
Blanket
Stroller

Place baby on his or her back on top of the blanket. Lie down next to baby on the blanket and wonder together. Look up at the sky, notice the color, and look for clouds. Move the blanket under a tree and look up at the tree branches and leaves. Visually explore the sky and all you see in it. Make up stories about the clouds as they float by. Make up songs about the birds and butterflies. Relax and enjoy the peace together.

Wit & Wisdom: Dissolve 1/2 cup baking soda in the bath to soothe skin irritations from insect bites, poison ivy, or itchy rashes.

—Rebecca D., Boulder, CO

Feel the Wind

Take baby outside today to feel all kinds of new sensations. Things that are ordinary to you will be brand new adventures for baby. If it's a warm summer day, feel the warmth of the sun. If there's a light rain, go out and feel the drops on your face. Let the wind blow through your hair, watch leaves float to the ground, or let snowflakes silently drift to the top of your tongue. Whatever the season, the outdoors offers endless possibilities. Smell a flower, walk barefoot through the grass, jump on a pile of leaves. Love of nature can be taught at a very young age and is communicated through a parent's enthusiasm, so enjoy your world!

Bird Watch

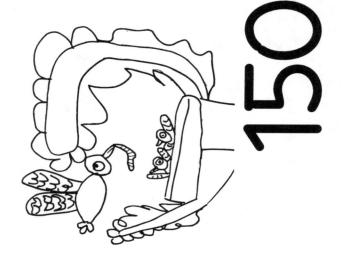

Materials
Pine cone
Peanut Butter
Bird seed

Make a bird feeder by rolling the pine cone first in peanut butter, then the bird seed. Hang the bird feeder by a string outside a window where it can be observed. Watch for birds to visit the feeder and encourage baby to watch when they do. Go to the library and check out a book on birds. Look through the book and see if you can identify the birds at your feeder. Talk about birds as you watch them eat.

What's That Smell?

151

Materials

Kitchen flavorings and spices
Foods that smell: salami, strawberries, yogurt, etc.
Perfumes, soaps, etc.
Flowers, grass, etc.

Make a game out of smelling the different flavorings, spices, foods, soaps, flowers, etc., around the house. As baby smells, tell them what they are smelling. If baby is old enough and already eating solid foods, let them taste the foods. It is fun to smell, and babies respond immediately to strong odors. Take baby out of the kitchen and go from room to room finding things for baby to smell. Continue the fun outdoors with flowers, grass, dirt, and anything else that might smell.

Plant a Seed

Materials
Bean seed
Paper cup
Dirt

Plant the bean in a paper cup. Help baby to water the seed when needed. Children are excited when something actually grows! Remember, even before children talk, they observe. Make sure they know the growing plant belongs to them, and point it out to other family members as well.

Nature Museum Display

Materials
Boxes from large matches
Cotton in a sheet
Piece of cardboard large enough to glue all
the boxes onto

Glue matchboxes onto the cardboard. Put cotton in the bottom of each box. Decide together what you want to display: rocks, sea shells, leaves, bark, feathers, etc. Then go on a walk to begin gathering for your museum. You may not be able to find everything on one walk, since this is a collection that may take time to complete. Display it someplace where everyone in the family can see it. Your child will be proud to play show and tell with what has been found!

153

Sand Cake

Materials
Sand
Dirt
Leaves, grass, rocks, twigs, and flowers

Form the sand or dirt into a pile to be the base for your sand cake. To make the cake, have your child collect nature's ingredients and stick them into the cake wherever they want. The cake ends up being a sculpture of twigs and leaves. Have pretend tea and cake together, complementing baby on his or her fabulous creation!

Centerpiece

When you go out for a walk today, collect things like flowers, rocks, twigs, branches, bark, or feathers. When you get home, arrange all the things you found in some sort of vase-like container or box. Put your display in the middle of the table where everyone eats. Tonight at dinner bring attention to the beautiful center-piece, pointing out all the different things that were collected. Even a one year old will know they had something to do with the display and feel proud to be part of it!

Moon Watch

Materials
Black construction paper
White chalk or paint

Go outside one night per week for a month and look at the moon. Help your child to draw the shape that is seen. Point out how the moon's shape changes each day. Looking at the sky at night creates a peaceful feeling, so enjoy these moments together. Young children often wonder why the moon follows them. Try answering that question!

Wit & Wisdom: My youngest child's favorite thing to do in the dark at night is to pretend to blow out the flashlight. He blows it just like a candle, and as he blows, I turn off the light.

—*Stacey Shiffman, Studio City, CA*

156

Bug Trap

Materials

Large yogurt container
Piece of cheese
4 two inch round rocks
8 inch square of heavy cardboard or board
Magnifying glass (optional)

Dig a hole in the ground large enough to fit the yogurt container in. Put a piece of cheese in the container. Place the four rocks at four corners on the dirt around the top of the yogurt container, then place the board on top, making sure the board doesn't touch the top of the yogurt container. Bugs will crawl in smelling the cheese and not be able to get out. Check your trap each day, looking at the bugs, then letting them go. If you don't have time to set a trap, go outside with your child with a sugar cube and magnifying glass. Place the cube on the ground and in a few minutes many ants will appear. Watch them through the magnifying glass.

Tree and Leaf Rubbings

Materials
Masking tape
Paper
Crayons

Take baby outside with the tape, paper, and crayons. Tape the paper to a tree and gently rub the crayon, using the long side not the tip, across the bark. Use different colored crayons and try different trees to see if the design changes. Look around for interesting leaves. Put the leaves on a flat surface and tape the paper over them, then rub the crayon over the leaves. Sit down with baby and compare the patterns found on your various rubbings.

Egg Head

Materials
Cress seeds
Cotton balls
Egg shells
Empty egg carton
Felt markers

Using half an egg shell, draw a face with markers, then set the shell in the egg carton. Soak the cotton balls in water, then place them inside the egg shell. Sprinkle cress seeds on top of the cotton balls. Set them in a windowsill for a few days, making sure to keep the cotton moist. Soon hair will be growing out of the egg shell!

Wish on a Star

Materials
Books on stars
Glow-in-the-dark star stickers

Children are fascinated with stars. Read books about stars to baby, and teach them the song Twinkle, Twinkle Little Star. Above the crib or bed, stick up glow-in-the-dark stars. Plan a night to take baby for a walk outside, point out stars, and make up stories about how stars have guided people to far off places. Start the tradition of looking for a special star and making a wish on it.

Sunrise

Make a special plan to get up at sunrise (if you're not up already!). Plan to go outside and watch the sunrise together, then have a special breakfast. If you are up early nursing baby, take a sunrise walk. It is a special time of day, so quiet and fresh. Find a few children's poems or a Native American story about the sun and read it together. Remember, children learn to appreciate nature from their own experience of it.

Nature Walk

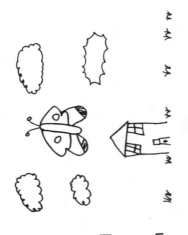

Materials
Large paper shopping bag
Items from nature
Scarf to use as a blindfold

Go outside together and gather nature's treasures such as feathers, leaves, grass, stones, bark, flowers, dirt, etc., and put them in the large paper bag. When you have at least ten things in the bag, sit down with baby and play the following guessing game. If baby wants to put the blindfold on do so, otherwise baby can close her eyes and reach her hand into the bag to feel one item at a time. As she brings the item out of the bag, you can describe what she is feeling. If baby has started talking, she may guess what the object is. After baby does this for a while, switch roles so the adult puts the blindfold on and reaches into bag to describe to baby what is being felt and guess what it is.

Dramatic
Play

Mr. Moon

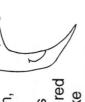

Materials
Two paper plates
Watercolor markers
Straws or popsicle sticks
Tape

On each plate draw a simple face with eyes, nose, mouth, eyebrows, and chin. One could be smiling, the other sad. Attach a straw or stick to the back of each with tape. Here is a sweet rhyme to say as you slowly and smoothly move the puppets for baby to watch:

Mr. Moon, Mr. Moon
You're up too soon.
The Sun's still high in the sky.
So go back to your bed,
and cover up your head,
and wait for the day to go by.

About three weeks after birth, baby is able to distinguish between colors. Warm colors such as yellow, orange, and red are preferred to cool ones like blue and green. By eight weeks, baby begins to focus both eyes to make a single, somewhat blurred image. At approximately four months old, baby can focus and see clearly, and really see what you look like in those early morning hours!

163

Horsey Ride

164

Materials
Several small bells
Ribbon or elastic

Sew or string bells onto the ribbon or elastic. Sit with baby in a rocker or comfortable chair and gently rock baby in your arms as you share this bouncing rhyme together.

Ride a cock horse to Banbury Cross
To see a fine lady (baby)
Upon a white horse. (change color of horse to black, brown, gray, etc.)
With rings on her (his) fingers (jingle bells on baby's fingers)
And bells on her (his) toes (jingle bells on toes)
She (he) shall have music wherever she (he) goes.
(Traditional, Great Britain)

Bouncing on the knee is especially fun for older babies.

It's Spider Time

Cradle baby in your arms or lie next to baby on the floor. Use your hands and arms to act out this classic story about a tenacious little spider who just can't kick the water spout habit. One hand is the spider crawling upward, the other washes over it like rain. Circle your arms up around your sunny face. If holding baby, use your available hand to act out the spider's part.

The eensy, weensy spider
climbed up the water spout.
Down came the rain and
washed the spider out.
Out came the sun and
dried up all the rain.
So the eensy, weensy spider
climbed up the spout again.

(Traditional, Great Britain, North America)

Ding-a-Ling

166

Materials
Toy telephone or real telephone no longer in use

Have a pretend conversation with someone special baby knows, like Grandma or Grandpa. Talk about something you and baby did that day. Then give baby a turn. You can say, "Grandma wants to talk with you too." Listen to the sounds and intonations baby makes while on the phone. Does baby sound like someone you know?

Wit & Wisdom: Every week my mother, who lived out of state, would send my daughter a page cut out of a coloring book for her to color in and send back. This carried on until my daughter went to kindergarten and it formed a very special bond.
—*Brooke M., Tucson, AZ*

Deep Sea Adventure

Materials
Laundry basket or box large enough to sit in
Jump rope
Paper towel tube (use as spyglass and bullhorn)
Small blanket

Pretend to go on a deep sea adventure with baby. Use hands to paddle your boat. Talk about creatures that live in the sea. Go for a swim (on the floor) kicking, paddling, and rolling around. Use your spyglass to search for land and the rope to tie up the boat. More props can be added, like fish shapes cut from cardboard and colored with markers. A child-size broom or plastic bat can act as an oar. The jump rope can be used for dramatic rescues with lots of pulling and tug-ging. Here's a rhyme to add spice to your adventure:

A sailor went to sea, sea, sea
To see what she could see, see, see
But all that she could see, see, see
Was the bottom of the deep blue sea,
sea, sea.

167

Under the Umbrella

Materials
Tin foil, umbrella, hula hoop, or towel

You don't have to wait for a real storm to go "singing in the rain" with baby. Pretend it's about to storm. Create interesting sound effects with tin foil and use your voice as the wind. Walk around together holding the umbrella (you may have to walk on your knees if baby wants to hold the umbrella), then sit under it and sing:

Rain, rain, go away,
Come again another day.
Little (baby's name) wants to play.
Rain, rain, go away.
(Traditional, Great Britain, North America)

Reach out from under the umbrella to feel the rain. It's stopped! Time for puddle jumping!

Say, "I'm going to jump in a puddle—follow me." Jump onto the towel, inside the hoop, or onto any imaginary puddle. Here's another rhyme to play with:

It's raining, it's pouring
The old man is snoring (substitute other
*   descriptive words, people, or animals—*
*   like "pink pig")*
He went to bed and he bumped his head
And he couldn't get up in the morning.
(Traditional, Great Britain, North America)

168

Over and Over

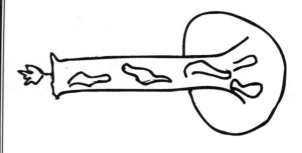

Materials
Birthday candle or other short candle
Playdough in small margarine tub (to hold candle)

When baby is ready to leave the ground with both feet, take turns jumping over the candlestick. You go first, then turn and give baby a boost over if needed. Explore different ways of getting over the candle, such as a big step over or crawling over on hands and feet.

Jack be nimble, Jack be quick,
Jack jump over the candlestick!
Jill be nimble, jump it too,
If Jack can do it, so can you!

Reprinted with permission from "Father Gander Nursery Rhymes," by Dr. Douglas W. Larche, published by Advocacy Press.

Finders Keepers

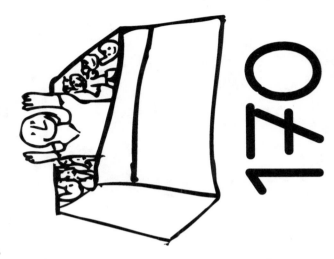

Materials
Clean box, large enough for baby to crawl into and play
Favorite toy or stuffed animal
Small blanket or beach towel
Flashlight

Tip box on its side and place favorite toy inside, then cover it with a blanket or towel. Say, "let's hunt for your (name of toy). I don't see it anywhere—where is it?" Encourage baby to hold flashlight and lead the way. Narrate as you search, using words that baby can attach to actions, such as behind, around, under, on top, over there, next to, and near. Of course, you both know where the toy is. The box could be a cave, house, castle, or airplane. If space in the box permits, drape a towel over the opening and, while baby is inside, peek your head in and make shadows on the side of the box with a flashlight.

Magic Carpet Ride

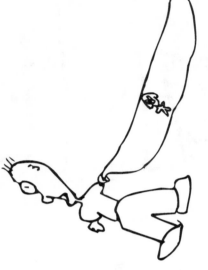

Materials
Sheet, quilt, blanket, or large beach towel
Toys baby chooses

Take baby on a magic carpet ride. Have baby sit or lie on the blanket, say the magic words and away you go. Say, "wave to your friends." When your arms get tired, rest and let baby take some toys for a ride. If blanket seems too big for baby to pull, provide something smaller for baby to pull. Some babies load up the blanket with as many toys as possible and then request another ride themselves!

Wit & Wisdom: The best way to wash stuffed animals is inside a pillowcase that is tied closed. That way the animals don't look worn after one washing.
—*Andrea G., Shorewood, MN*

Play Is Hard Work

Once baby is walking around, wandering, carrying, and dumping are preferred activities. Provide empty, sealed cereal and cracker boxes along with paper shopping bags for baby to play grocery. Small canned goods are fun because of their shape and weight. Bean bags, cardboard blocks, paper bags stuffed with newspaper and sealed with masking tape, lunch boxes, baskets, purses, and pillowcases are also versatile props for this type of play.

172

Mountain Bear

Materials
A mound of pillows and cushions to be a "mountain"

Pictures of bears, bear book, visit to zoo, public television program (some prior experience of what bears are like)

You and baby both be bears and pretend you're looking for blueberries to eat. Say or sing this silly song as you climb over the mountain:

Oh, the bear went over the mountain,
The bear went over the mountain,
The bear went over the mountain, to see what he could see.
And all that he could see, and all that he could see,

Was the other side of the mountain,
The other side of the mountain,
The other side of the mountain was all that he could see.

Think of other animals baby has seen and use your body and voice to act like them. Say, "what animal do you want to be?" wait for response, then suggest an animal with which baby is familiar.

What If?

Here are lots of ideas for creating imaginary situations with baby. Choose a character, then something that character does, and play make-believe with baby. Characters can include:

mommy
daddy
baby
any animal
musician in band
truck driver
hair dresser
pilot
doctor
dancer
circus performer

mail carrier
police officer
fire fighter
construction worker
farmer
salesperson
bus driver
animal trainer
veterinarian
orchestra conductor

food server
cook
grocery clerk
singer
office worker
teacher
train engineer
astronaut
nurse

A simple prop or two helps baby become the character. For example, if baby wants to play mail carrier and post office, use a shoebox for a mailbox, junk mail as "mail," and make a

mailbag out of a brown paper bag (cut off the top and use it to make a shoulder strap) or canvas tote bag. Toy instruments, medical kits, tools, and dishes are great for enriching baby's play. A bike helmet can double as an astronaut's helmet or a construction worker's hardhat. A plastic bat, plastic golf club, or yardstick stuffed between some couch cushions could be the stick shift of a forklift, truck, or bus. Let your imagination soar—and save those cardboard boxes.

Jack and Jill Cooperate

Materials
Child-size step stool
Small bucket or pail
Torn pieces of newspaper or blue
construction paper (for pretend water)

Jack and Jill went up the hill
To fetch a pail of water.
Jack fell down and broke his crown,
And Jill came tumbling after.

Jill and Jack went up the track
To fetch the pail again.
They climbed with care, got safely there,
And finished the job they began.

Reprinted with permission from "Father Gander
Nursery Rhymes," by Dr. Douglas W. Larche,
published by Advocacy Press.

Pretend the stool is a hill. Hold baby's hand
while baby steps up, then down, then tumble
and roll on the floor together. Repeat the song a
second time going over the stool, circling around
with the bucket and finishing the job together.

Here is another rhyme that's fun to recite
and even funnier to act out.

There was a little man who had a little
*   crumb*
and over the mountain he did run,
With a belly full of fat,
And a big tall hat,

And a pancake stuck to his
bum, bum, bum.
(Traditional, Great Britain, North America)

175

Dress-Up Box

Look through your closet for things you don't wear or want anymore: hats, gloves, slippers, shoes, belts, shirts, and pants. Find a big box and paint the outside or buy a special "dress-up" container. Put all your discarded items into the new dress-up box. Let other people know you are looking for fun dress-up clothes. Antique stores, thrift stores, and garage sales are good places to look. Keep your collection going and take time often to play dress-up with your baby. Make sure to hold baby in front of a mirror to see how you both look.

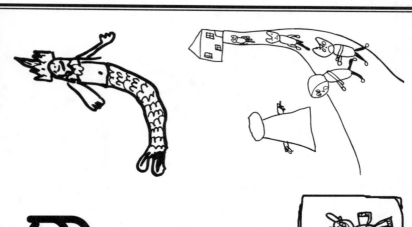

Storytelling

Moon Glow

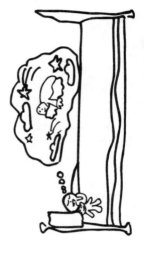

On a clear night when the moon is full, take baby in your arms and bask in its glow together. The moon's shape and brightness will draw baby's eyes to it like a magnet. Share your feelings about the moon with baby. It is truly a natural wonder worth telling a story about. Consider these as possible story starters:

The moon is like a giant ball…
See the face on the moon…
The moon is many miles away…
The moon has many secrets to tell…
We could fly there some day…

Baby's first word just might be "moon."

Do I Have One for you

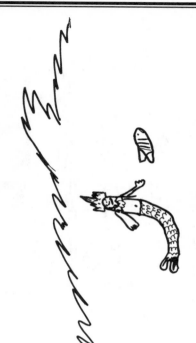

178

We all have stories to tell and they come from various sources. Some are from our dreams, some from our memory, some from people we've known, or books we've read. A few we simply imagine! Well, there's no time like the present to relax, clear your head of the day's events and think about your life experiences, people, pets, places lived, fears, favorite things, wishes you had or have, and family traditions. As you take this journey into your memory, bring back something to share with baby. Tell it as you remember, or change it to what you want to communicate today. You create the story. Stories grow and change over time with the telling. Much can be learned about yourself, and at the same time, baby is learning to love language and the art of storytelling.

Young Collector

There are many types of books to choose from, whether you're borrowing from the library or purchasing from a bookstore. Look for these sure-to-please types:

- Nursery rhymes
- Song picture books
- Books with predictable, repetitive patterns
- Different shaped books
- Chunky board books
- Vinyl books
- Peek-a-boo books
- Books with textures
- Big books

Books that have something to do with baby's real-life experiences are favorites. Those with clear, colorful pictures showing babies playing, eating, sleeping, bathing, crying, being held, or going on outings like the grocery, park, swimming pool, beach, or library are favorites. Books with animals, trucks, trains, flowers, and trees are also favored. With time, you'll know which books baby treasures—they'll be well-worn from repeated reading (and chewing).

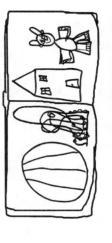

179

Seeing Is Believing

180

Baby learns to read by being surrounded by language, seeing others read, and being read to. At first, baby will lie or sit on your lap, enjoying the closeness and sound of your voice. Then baby will become actively interested in the books themselves: touching, smelling, and tasting, as well as looking at them. Baby may hit the pages in excitement, then point at pictures, turn the pages, and eventually babble about the pictures. Let baby "read" you their favorite story. Your attention and enthusiasm will make reading and sharing books so rewarding for baby that they will learn to truly love books!

Moving Story

choo choo

181

As baby starts to move around, stories that invite acting out and participation are great fun. When it's hard for baby to sit still, choose a book that really moves. Something with a character that is doing something baby could do. Remember, a book doesn't have to be read non-stop from cover to cover to be enjoyed. It's OK to set it down and roll, jump, hide, crawl, giggle, clap, stomp, and chomp. Make your own moving story with pictures from magazines. For instance, a picture of a puppy, the beach, some children, a bus, or a train could be made into a story about a puppy looking for mischief who leaves its yard, follows some children who get on a bus that happens to be going to the beach, and so on. The possibilities are endless.

All Stuffed Up

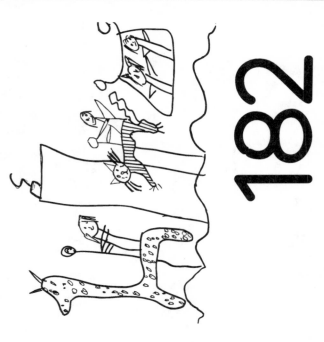

Babies have a knack for attracting large quantities of stuffed animals, dolls, and creatures of unknown origin. Put them to use by casting them in stories you tell. They don't have to be a puppet to be used like one. If you happen to have toys that are similar, such as two teddy bears, bunnies, kittens, etc., then you have a family. Some themes are more popular than others depending on baby's personality and stage of development. Favorites may include getting lost, then found, going on a journey, driving different vehicles, climbing hills to find something, looking for mother, going to the zoo, birthday parties, and being in a parade. Take your cue from baby.

Trip Story

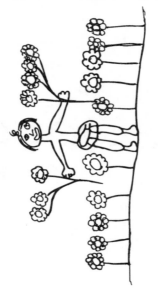

Go on an outing with baby: a walk around the block, a trip to the pet store, a visit to a neighbor, out to pick flowers, or anything else that interests both of you. Make sure as you walk to point out interesting things along the way. When you get home, get out a large piece of paper or open a paper grocery bag and begin drawing. Make a picture map, telling baby what you did together as you draw. Start at your front door and draw everything from that point until you returned home. Use simple stick drawings or scribbles if need be. As baby gets older, she can tell you what she did and you can draw it. Later, baby can draw as well. Remember, her drawing may not resemble anything. However, she might put down a scribble, and know exactly what it is! Let her tell you what she sees—it will be fun for both of you!

183

Draw and Tell

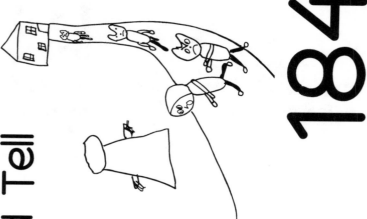

Materials
Piece of white paper
Crayons

Think of a short, simple story either made up or from a book. Get out the piece of paper, and as you tell it from memory, draw the story. Simple stick figures or scribbles will do. As you draw things mentioned in the story, a scene will take shape. Color things in as you go. Make up a story about baby—he will love a story about himself. As baby gets older, let him tell you a story as you draw or let him draw as you tell a story.

Collage Story

Materials
Old magazine
Scissors
Glue
Piece of paper

Look through magazines together. If baby points to a picture or seems interested, cut it out. Glue the pictures onto the paper. Once all the pictures are glued on, make up a story about them. Change the story a few times, starting with a different picture, then adding the others to the story's plot. Since baby picked the pictures, she will feel a great sense of involvement and pride in her homemade story.

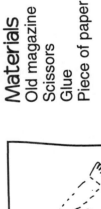

Shadow Stories

Shadows are fascinating to watch and fun to form. All you need is light (a flashlight will do) and a flat, light-colored surface, like a wall. The stronger the light and the whiter the flat surface, the clearer the shadow picture will be. Change the size of the shadows by moving your hands closer to the light or farther away. One of the simplest shadows to cast is a rabbit. You do this by holding two fingers up in a peace sign. Experiment using one hand, then use one hand with the other hand over the top or underneath. Experiment further by adding features to animals, like a snail, turtle, dog, goose, moose, alligator, crab, and bird. Make up your own stories and rhymes to go with the shadows you create: *there was a tiny snail that moved so slow, she came out when it rained to stretch and grow, she nibbled on leaves and all the yellow flowers, even though it rained and rained for hours.* Have fun with words and you'll surprise yourself!

Tree Home Stories

Materials
Brown cardboard box (you can use more than one and stack them)
Wrapping paper tubes or paper towel tubes
Masking tape
Stuffed animals or puppets

Cut an oval-shaped hole in one side of the cardboard box as the entrance of the tree home. The size of the oval depends on who's going to be living in the tree! Use the tubes to make branches by taping them onto the box or cutting a hole in the box and sticking one end of the tube into it. There are many animals that live in trees to choose from for storytelling: raccoon, bear, owl, squirrel, mouse, and more. Choose an animal you already have in stuffed form, or make one from a sock with buttons, cloth, permanent marker, construction paper, yarn, or felt. Look at pictures with baby of different animals that live in tree homes. Talk about what they eat and how they stay warm. Lastly, create a story about your animal.

Clay and Playdough

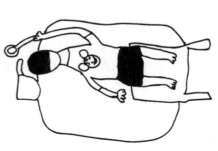

Everyday Playdough

Ingredients
2 cups flour
1 cup salt
1 teaspoon cream of tartar
2 tablespoons oil
1 teaspoon food coloring
2 cups water

Playdoughs provide hours of fun by giving busy, growing little hands something to do. Below is a recipe for a smooth, pliable dough. It can be stored in a plastic container for several weeks, and does not need to be refrigerated.

Mix the above ingredients in a saucepan over medium heat, stirring constantly, until dough leaves sides of pan. Continue to stir dough ball around in the pan for a minute, then remove it from pan and knead for several minutes. Once cool, explore texture of dough with baby: squish, roll, pound, press, cut (with dull plastic knife), twist, tear, make prints. Check the bottom of your feet and baby's feet before you walk to other areas. Playdough has a way of getting around!

188

Another Dough,
No Cooking Required!

Ingredients
4 cups flour
1 cup iodized salt
1 3/4 cups warm water

Mix ingredients in a bowl and knead for ten minutes. Shape dough into small figures or globs. If you wish to keep some of baby's sculptures, they can be baked at 300°F until hard. Hand and footprints are sweet keepsakes.

189

Puff Dough

Ingredients
3 cups flour
1 cup salt
3 tablespoons oil
1 cup water

Mix flour and salt in a mixing bowl. Stir in oil and water. Add more water as needed to form soft, puffy dough. This dough is great for playing bakery. A small apron, rolling pin, and cupcake pan will go a long way toward entertaining baby.

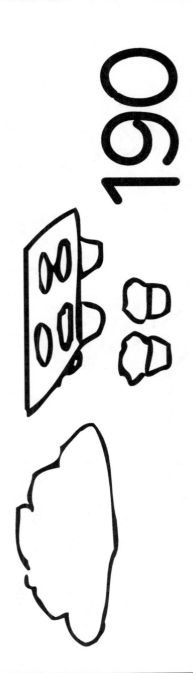

190

Tea Party Dough

You can eat this dough—really!

Ingredients
1 cup peanut butter
1 cup corn syrup
1 1/2 cups powdered sugar
1 1/2 cups powdered milk

Mix ingredients together in a mixing bowl and knead. Additional powdered milk may be needed to make the dough less sticky. Use cookie cutters or design your own shapes and have a little tea party. If the tea party idea doesn't fly, try having a birthday party. Birthday candles are fun to stick in dough.

Gooey Goop

Ingredients
1 cup cornstarch
1 cup water
Square cake pan or large tub
Bowl, spoon, plastic or metal measuring
  cups, funnel

Mix cornstarch with water and pour into a
pan or large tub. Goop it up with safe,
interesting kitchen gadgets: slotted spoon,
whisk, basting brush, salad tongs, etc.
Goop has a completely different texture
than dough, but like playdough, it is fun to
hide things in!

192

Super Stretch Dough

Ingredients
2 bowls and plastic container with lid
2 cups white glue
1 1/2 cups water
Food coloring
1/3 cup water (2 times)
1 teaspoon borax (2 times)

Mix white glue, several drops of food color, and
1 1/2 cups water in a bowl. In the other bowl,
mix 1/3 cup water with the borax, then stir it into glue mixture. A blob
will form that you pull out and place in a plastic container. Knead it
slightly. To the remaining glue mixture, add water and borax
again. Stir and pull out another blob, combining it with the
first in the plastic container. This dough can go the distance.
It will stretch, loop, spiral, braid, wiggle, cut, roll, and
spread. Watch what happens if you and baby leave it on the
table in a ball and come back a few minutes later.

193

Old Fashioned Fun

194

Ingredients
Dirt and water = MUD
Outdoor work area
Bucket or hose
Small shovel or spoon

Find a place in the yard or playground where there is "clean" dirt; garden areas are ideal. Loosen a two to three foot area with the shovel. Add water from a hose or bucket and mix it all up with your hands, spade, shovel, spoon, stick, or other tools. Make some slooshy, squooshy, mush. Smack, stir, pull, and push something special together. You can place your creations on cookie sheets, plastic lids, or a piece of wood. Decorate with sand, grass, pebbles, flower petals, and twigs. This can also be done inside if you have a large tub and don't mind cleaning up.

Cornmeal Dough

Ingredients
1 1/2 cups flour
1 1/2 cups cornmeal
1 cup salt
1 cup water
Bowl or plastic container with lid

Mix all the ingredients in a bowl. Add more water to form a smooth dough. Dough will last several weeks in an airtight container. As with other dough, explore texture, roll, and shape. Use different kitchen gadgets and other household objects to make imprints: keys, combs, straws, forks, and various cookie cutters.

195

Cornstarch Dough

Ingredients
1/2 cup salt
1/2 cup hot water
1/4 cup cold water

1/2 cup cornstarch
Pan, bowl, and board

Mix salt with hot water and boil in the pan. Stir cold water into cornstarch in the bowl. Add cornstarch mixture to boiling water and stir. Cook over low heat, stirring until mixture resembles pie dough. Remove and turn onto a board. When cool, knead until smooth.

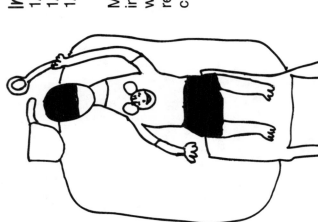

Clay Works

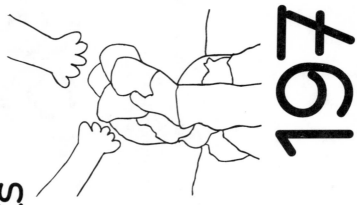

Go to your nearest art supply store and buy a big bag of clay. Clay feels different from play-dough. It is much denser and is slippery when water is applied. You can sculpt it with your hands as well as rocks, sticks, or wooden clay tools. Using a string or butter knife, remove a chunk of clay from the bag. A pillowcase makes a good surface on which to model. It can be folded up afterward and used each time the clay is brought out. Fill a small container with water and show baby how to dip fingertips into the water, rubbing them on the clay. Pinch the clay to make shapes. The clay will dry hard if left out for a few days, but will be very break-able. Baby will like to show everyone his work of art!

Water Play

String of Floaters

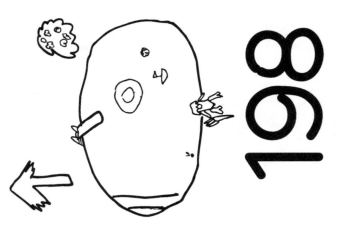

Materials
Styrofoam (from meat trays, box packing, etc.)
Corks
Sponges
Small, thin wood pieces
Lightweight string

Cut the Styrofoam or sponge into shapes. Poke holes in the Styrofoam, sponges, wood, and corks. Thread the string through the hole in each of the objects. Tie the ends of the string together so that the objects are hanging like a necklace. Put the string of floaters in the bath, lake, river, or in an outside wading pool.

Wit & Wisdom: Put food color in water, then pour into ice cube trays. Dump frozen ice cubes into bath. Baby will have so much fun trying to pick them up!

—Toni T., Salinas, CA

Bubbles and Waves

Materials
Kitchen egg beater
Wire whisks, spoons, etc.
Straws or plastic tubing
Floating boat or block

Put together a bucket of fun for bathtub play. Place the boat or toy in the water. Use the egg beater to create waves behind the boat, making the boat move through the water. The straw or tubing can be used to blow bubbles. Get a second piece of tubing long enough so you can enjoy blowing bubbles from outside the bath. The spoons and whisk can be used for splashing. The idea is to make bathtime fun and make water a friend.

Wit & Wisdom:
Put a bath towel down on the bottom of the tub; that way baby can lie on their back and kick as much as they want without sliding. Of course, make sure there are only a few inches of water in the bath.

—Todd P., St. Cloud, MN

199

Learn to Pour

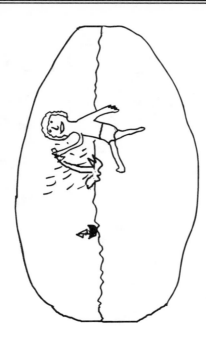

200

Materials
Containers of all sizes
Bathtub or small wading pool

There is no better place for baby to experience pouring than in the bathtub. Babies love to fill things up and dump them out. As they get older, they may begin pouring from one container to another. Watching the water flow and splash is sure to bring giggles.

Wit & Wisdom: Use a handheld shower attachment and put it under the water to create a whirlpool effect. It's really fun when there are bubbles growing.
—Martha B., Columbus, OH

Pavement Painting

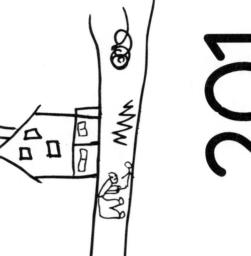

Materials
Old paintbrushes
Bucket
Piece of blacktop, cement, or wood decking

Fill the bucket with water and bring it outside. Dip paintbrushes in water and start painting on the pavement. Baby will love making a shape, then seeing it disappear as the sun dries the pavement. There is no mess to clean up, water is free, and baby will be entertained for at least a while!

Wit & Wisdom: If baby has colic, take the car seat from the car, put the baby in it, and put it on top of the dryer. Turn it on. The dryer is warm and simulates a car's motion. Soon colicky baby is fast asleep!

—*Jan Collins, Edina, MN*

Dish Washing

What better water activity than washing plastic dishes in the kitchen sink! Put dishwashing soap in the sink to create lots of bubbles. Put a safe, sturdy stool next to the sink and let baby go to town. They can use the dish brush that you use and set the clean dishes on a towel. They can even dry them and put them away in their play kitchen or toy box. This will give baby something to do while you are cooking dinner!

Wit & Wisdom: Punch holes in the bottom of a plastic container and fill it with water. Baby will enjoy watching the water spray through the holes.

—*Mary W., Atlanta, GA.*

202

Wiggle Slide

Materials
Large plastic sheet, 12 feet or longer (can use cut plastic garbage bag)
Hose with a sprinkler
Grass to put plastic sheet on

Put the plastic sheet outside on the grass and turn on the hose or sprinkler. Get your bathing suit on and join baby for a wet wiggling experience. Once babies can crawl they will love this wet, slippery, sliding experience. Older toddlers will run and slide on the plastic, so make sure that baby is out of the way. Hold on to baby and pull him toward you on his stomach, lie on your backs and squirm, make like an angel in the snow and move your arms up and down. On a hot day nothing beats sprinkler fun!

Wit & Wisdom:
When my two year old started slamming doors, I would jump out of my chair in fright. Another mother suggested I put towels over the top of the doors. Now I don't worry about little fingers, or noise.

—*Lizza R., Chesterland, OH*

203

Rub-a-Dub Scrub

Two fun and easy-to-remember rhymes to splash around to are:

Rub-a-dub-dub, three folks in a tub (rub baby's tummy)
And who do you think they be?
The butcher, the baker, the candlestick maker (count 1-2-3 on fingers)
They've all gone off on a spree! (hide fingers in fist)

*****

I had a little turtle, his name was Tiny Tim,
I put him in the bathtub, to see if he could swim,
He drank up all the water, he ate up all the soap,
And now he's sick in bed, with bubbles in his throat.
Bubble, bubble, bubble, glub.

Wit & Wisdom: Give baby a soft, small washcloth to hold in the bath. The texture feels good on baby's hands and gums.

—*Cheryl W., Lancaster, PA*

204

Bubbles for Baby

Older babies can blow their own bubbles using slotted spoons, plastic berry baskets, or store-bought bubble wands.

Materials
Mild recipe
1/3 cup tearless baby shampoo
1 1/4 cups water
2 teaspoons sugar
1 drop food coloring

Strong, thick recipe
1/4 cup clear liquid dishwashing detergent
1/4 cup glycerin (from drugstore)
3/4 cup water
1 tablespoon sugar

Combine the ingredients and pour the bubble solution into an unbreakable container with a lid. Blow bubbles for baby to wonder at. Encourage baby to try to catch bubbles in the air. Which ones catch baby's eye?

Happy Helper

Baby loves to help around the house, and jobs that involve water are a big hit. Pour two tablespoons white vinegar into a small spray bottle and fill it with water. Show baby how to spray the window, then polish it with a paper towel. When you finish the windows, how about the floor? Put about four inches of warm soapy water into a cleaning bucket (one or two drops of mild liquid dish soap will do). Put two sponges in the bucket and work together on a small area. Show baby how to squeeze the extra water out of the sponge before putting it on the floor. Baby may or may not care whether the floor resembles a large puddle, but he will derive great satisfaction from working with you.

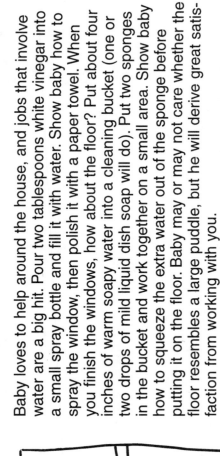

206

Some Float, Some Don't

Materials
Clear plastic container or tub
Variety of household items: sponge, clothespin, spoon, key, plastic toy, cup, wood block, comb, shell, paper, etc.
Beach towel

Spread towel out on the floor over a low table, or outside if the weather is warm. Fill the container two-thirds full with water and place it on the towel. Set the items you have chosen on the towel next to the container. Baby will probably begin putting the items into the water without much prompting from you. Say, "Let's see which things stay on top of the water and which things fall to the bottom." Use the words "float" and "sink" as you notice where each item

is, and talk about what they're made of: wood, metal, plastic, sponge, etc. Remember, the questions you ask out loud are to encourage baby to think scientifically and develop observation skills; don't worry whether the answer is right or wrong. Encourage observation of life!

207

Rainbow Surprise

When the sun shines after a rain shower, sometimes our eyes are treated to a beautiful rainbow. Seven colors appear in every rainbow: red, orange, yellow, green, blue, indigo, and violet. Most of the time only four or five colors can be seen clearly. An enjoyable wet activity to do on a sunny day is to create your own rainbow. If the weather is very warm, bathing suits are a must. Turn on the garden hose, adjust the nozzle to the fine spray setting, then arch the water high into the air. Watch with baby as the rays of the sun hit the water and create a rainbow. Talk about the different colors you see as you experiment moving the hose around. This can also be done with a sprinkler if it is put in the right spot. Find a rainbow story from the library and share it with baby. If a hose is not available, try using a plastic squeeze bottle filled with water.

208

Freeze for All

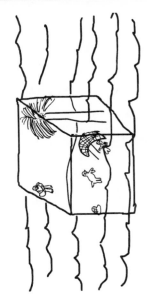

Materials
Clean paper milk carton, quart or half-gallon size
Small plastic figures of zoo animals and sea life

Fill the milk carton with water and several small figures. Place it in the freezer until frozen solid. When it is frozen, remove the ice block from the carton and place it in a plastic tub for baby to explore. Touch the ice with baby and talk about what you feel. Slide objects on the surface. For baby's bath, place the block into the bathtub. Watch what happens as the ice slowly melts. Is the bath water surrounding the block cooler? Can baby see what's inside the block? During summer months, ice blocks large and small are fun to play with outside. Baby learns how water changes shape and magically evaporates.

Parks and Recreation

Just Strolling Through

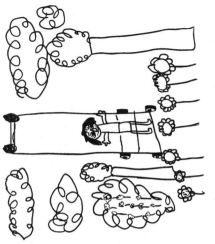

210

When baby seems to nap often, and you feel the need for exercise and fresh air, visit park areas with paved walking and bike paths. Make sure your stroller is designed to accommodate a newborn baby: it should recline, be well padded, have an awning, a safety belt, and meet all federal safety standards. Take an extra diaper and wipes, water, baby blanket, sun protection, a snack, and away you both go. If much of your day is spent alone with baby, this might be a great time to meet a friend and walk together.

Wit & Wisdom: To keep your baby wipes moist, turn them upside down once in a while so all the moisture doesn't sit at the bottom.
—*Alice W., San Carlos, CA*

Breakfast Club

Baby loves to go out almost as much as you do. Many parks have wonderful lawn areas where you can put down a blanket and relax. But make sure they didn't just turn off the sprinklers! On beautiful days when you can't wait to get outside, don't wait until lunchtime to have a picnic. Pack a continental breakfast, blanket, small underinflated beachball, and a favorite toy and head for the park. After breakfast, play with the ball and lie on your backs staring up at the great big sky.

211

A Place to Park

Stop by your city parks and recreation department and ask if they have a park directory. If not, go exploring on your own. Keep a small notebook describing the facility for future reference. You will soon discover all parks are not the same. Some are older, with metal play structures, and in need of repair, while others are brand new and made of wood and plastic. Some have baby swings and areas specially designed for babies and small children, while others are geared more for the school age child. Things to consider when checking out parks include:

- Do you feel safe there?
- Are there bathrooms?
- Are there working water fountains?
- Is the park kept clean?

- Is there shade for sunny days?
- What types of activities is that park used for?
- Are pets allowed?
- What is the play equipment like?

212

Swing Rhythm

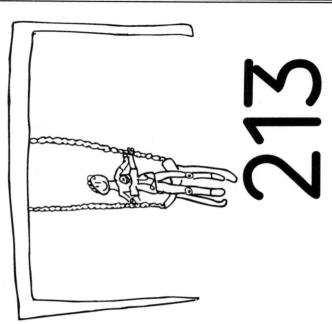

Some babies could swing the whole day through. Until baby is able to hold up his head, swing together gently on the big swings. When baby's neck and head are strong enough, introduce the baby swing. A rolled up baby blanket makes a nice cushion around baby and fills in some of the extra space inside the baby swing. Push baby gently from the front so you can look at each other—you'll know when baby has had enough. Gently squeeze baby's feet when the swing comes toward you. Hide your face with your hands and say "boo" as you lean in to push. Simply sitting in the swing and kicking his legs is great fun for baby. As baby grows and becomes an accomplished baby swinger, you may hear the words, "high, high, high." That means keep on pushing!

Ready for Anything

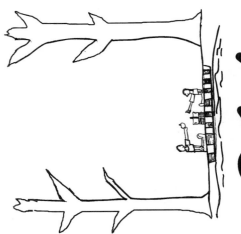

Make a park kit to keep in your house or car which is full of special, practical things that will make your trips to the park more carefree and fun. Purchase or find a large canvas tote or a shopping bag with handles. Fill it with things that are "must-haves" on almost all outings to the park:

- Blanket or large beach towel
- First-aid kit
- Sunscreen
- A few paper bags for collecting things
- Sand toys, such as a pail, shovel, funnel, sifter, vehicles, and small toy animals
- Extra diapers and wipes
- Umbrella for rain or shine
- Magnifying glass for investigating

Add to this list as you discover what your park needs are. Having a kit like this makes going to the park much easier to prepare for.

214

The Sandbox Scene

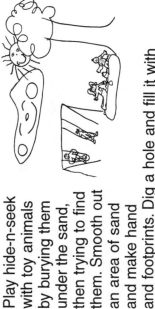

A well-planned sandy area at a park is a great place for baby to explore. There are endless possibilities and only one rule to remember: don't throw sand! While baby is practicing digging, filling, and pouring, she also will have opportunities to watch other babies playing. Baby's first attempts at socializing outside the family just might occur in the sandbox. Some useful items for sandplay include:

- Shoebox to fill and dump
- Frozen juice containers for filling and making towers
- Sand shovel, spoons, ice cream scooper
- Measuring cups
- Variety of vehicles and plastic figures

Make a hill of sand with baby. Pat it down all around, then, starting at opposite sides, dig through trying to reach each other's hands.

Play hide-n-seek with toy animals by burying them under the sand, then trying to find them. Smooth out an area of sand and make hand and footprints. Dig a hole and fill it with water, then watch the water disappear. If the weather is warm, bury each other's feet.

215

Anticipate Problems

Curiosity and determination can land baby in situations that are more challenging than baby is physically ready for. Always be alert and anticipate situations where baby may need your help or words of warning. Areas to watch closely are:

- Swings: they don't have brakes and children using them are not always watching for curious babies.

- Don't assume older children at the park will be careful around baby. Many don't even notice and are simply not aware.

- If the park is busy, remove baby from the bottom of the slide so the next child's feet don't end up in baby's back.

- Babies love merry-go-rounds, both to ride on and to watch. They will not wait for it to stop before trying to hitch a ride, so you must be close enough to hold baby back. Be sure to warn them of the danger.

Accidents do happen, but fewer happen when baby is carefully supervised.

216

Tree Love

Help baby develop an appreciation for the unique living things that are found in many outdoor parks by choosing a special tree to be a friend. Choose a tree at a park you go to frequently. Introduce baby to the tree (call it "tree") and say what kind it is (if you know or have looked it up). Give the tree a great big hug! Talk about the tree's trunk, branches, leaves, and anything else about the tree you notice. Give the tree a good-bye hug when you're ready to leave the park. Repeat this each time you see your tree and talk with baby about any seasonal changes you notice.

Hi Kites

Materials
Markers
Paper plates
Crepe paper streamers
Tape
String, twine, or yarn

Long before baby is able to fly a kite on their own, they will be fascinated with kites when they see them flying in the sky. Parks with large, open, grassy areas tend to attract kite flyers. Help baby make a kite to hold and run with. Attach a string to the back of a paper plate with tape, or poke two holes near the center, run the string through, and knot it. Baby can hold one edge of the plate and run with it. Tape on colorful streamers for the kite's tail. This kind of kite doesn't fly high in the sky, it simply blows in the wind behind baby. Plain crepe paper cut into streamers are fun to wave in the wind by themselves. Draw designs or a face on the plate to decorate. Make two and you both can go fly a kite!

218

Tiny Treasure Hunt

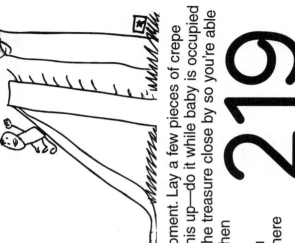

Materials
Sand shovel or spoon
Crepe paper
Coffee can, cookie tin, or small shoebox
Costume jewelry (anything treasure-like)

Place jewelry in a container and hide it under some leaves, near a bush, behind a tree, or in a small hole covered with sand or dirt. Create a paper trail by tying crepe paper around or onto trees, bushes, and play equipment. Lay a few pieces of crepe paper on the ground too. You have to be sneaky setting this up—do it while baby is occupied with a toy in the sand or swinging in a baby swing. Hide the treasure close by so you're able to see baby at all times in case baby needs your help. When you and baby are ready, say, "let's go on a treasure hunt, paper marks the trail." Pick up the paper as you go. If you like, make up a story about pirates leaving the treasure there a long time ago.

219

Five, Six, Pick-Up Sticks

Materials
Pail, paper bag, or shoebox

Use a pail to help baby collect interesting nature items. Twigs, sticks, wood chips, leaves, sand, shells, pebbles, and nuts are all fair game as baby explores the park. Once collected, dump everything on a smooth surface and encourage baby to talk about the collection. Which stick or pebble is the biggest? Which is the smallest? Are some things smooth, rough, wet, or dry? Arrange and rearrange your found items with baby according to the characteristics of what you find.

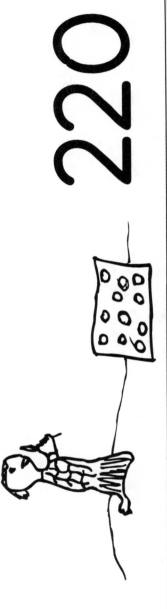

220

What's Yours Is Mine

Park time with baby can be frustrating if your baby continually wanders over to other babies nearby, sits down next to them, and begins playing with their toys. At this stage, baby thinks that they can have everything they see, and they want to explore everything around them. Here are a few tips to make park play easier:

- Practice going to the park with another parent and child to teach your baby how to share with another baby without grabbing things.

- Approach any mother at the park and introduce yourself to break the ice. Then both of you can help direct the babies' play. Make sure you bring toys to the park that your baby likes to play with. They can then take one of their own toys to show the other baby.

- Wrap one of baby's old toys they haven't seen for a while in bright paper and give it to them as a surprise.

After a few trips to the park, both you and baby will have made a few new friends.

221

Celebrations

Neighborhood Welcome

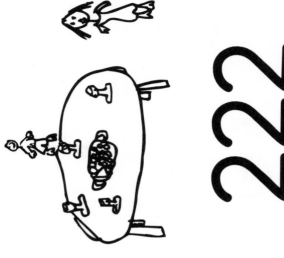

There may be new mothers in your neighborhood you have never met. How fun it would be to invite them over for tea and snacks. Pick a date for your welcome tea and write up a little flier inviting all mothers with children under five years to attend. Put the flier in the mailboxes near your house. Hire a baby-sitter to watch the children so the mothers can visit. Name tags are a must for the children and the mothers. Put a notebook out for everyone to list their name, address, phone number, children's names and ages, and whether they would be interested in meeting to play regularly at someone's home or a park. Think about the resource mothers can be for each other. This could lead to a neighborhood child care co-op, car pool possibilities, resources for doctors, baby-sitters, etc. Most of all, it is important to have friends that live close who can be supportive. Send a copy of the name list to each person after the event.

222

Baby Sleeps All Night

Celebrate baby sleeping through the night for the first time. The day after the big sleep, plan to have a night walk as a family. Night is a mysterious and beautiful time with many new sounds. It is an adventure everyone can look forward to, especially big brothers and sisters. Bring a thermos of hot chocolate and a blanket so everyone can stop and sit somewhere to look at the stars. The fresh air will most likely guarantee baby will repeat the previous night by sleeping until morning! Sweet dreams....

223

Sibling Party

When baby is one month old, invite other mothers with young children your older child's age over for a celebration. Make sure all babies are left at home and that the new baby in your house is being looked after by someone else. Plan games according to the ages of children attending (see the Baby-Sitting and Playgroup chapter for game ideas). Focus on the baby's siblings. Point out to them that the reason for the celebration is that they are so special. All children should receive a prize of some sort. Have fun with the older child, making no mention of baby at all.

Baby's Birthday

Baby might not understand what a birthday is until their second or third year, but they will certainly feel the excitement of something special happening to them if any of the following events happen:

1. Before baby wakes, maybe even the night before, decorate baby's room with balloons, streamers, confetti, etc.

2. Put a present in baby's bed so upon awakening baby can open it. If baby is too young to open it, leave a rattle or toy with bright ribbon around it.

3. Buy a plain white sheet to be used as a birthday tablecloth. Have all the guests sign it in permanent ink. This sheet can be washed and used year after year.

4. Have each member of the family write any events that happened during baby's first year. Save this for baby's scrapbook.

5. Serve assorted baby food for dinner. Baby will laugh to see everyone eating the same thing as they are.

Birthday Theme Ideas

Babies that are age one and two will enjoy having a party with other children, as long as no one plays with their toys, and you have a parent attending for each child. It can be fun to have a theme party, which means all the games, decorations, food, etc., follow the same idea. Here are a few baby themes:

Trains, Trucks, Buses, or Planes: Decorations could be toys or trucks. Have everyone make a shoebox train and pull it around. Babies could get conductor hats as party favors, and the cake could represent a wheel.

Balls: All the games could have to do with balls. For an invitation, write the party information on a small rubber ball and give it to the child.

Dolls: Decorate in tea party fashion and have each child bring a doll. Serve small sandwiches the dolls can share and tea served in tiny cups. Give a piece of doll clothing as a party favor. Make a cake using a rounded jelly mold, then stick an old Barbie in it. Then decorate the cake like a skirt.

Blocks: Have games based around building with blocks. Use big cardboard blocks and boxes to make an obstacle course or fort for babies to play in. Even the cake can be cut, stacked, and iced to look like blocks.

226

Pass the Parcel

Materials
Candy   Wrapping paper
Small gifts   Music

Children of all ages love playing this game at parties and celebrations. Wrap up one prize or candy. Then wrap another one over the top of the first. Keep adding gifts and candy in layers until you have one large parcel. When it's time to play, everyone sits in a circle (if babies are very small, parents can hold them on their laps). Someone needs to be in charge of the music. Turn the music on and begin passing the parcel. When it has gone around at least once, turn the music off. Whoever is holding the parcel gets to open one layer of paper, getting a prize. The music person needs to make sure that everyone gets at least one prize.

Wit & Wisdom: Write invitations for baby's party on balloons, then deflate them and send them in the mail. They will have to blow up the balloons to get the news!

—*Clara S., Worcester, MA*

227

Baby Things Exchange Party

Invite all your friends and neighbors over for an informal exchange of unwanted baby things. Items could include clothes, books, toys, blankets, crib or room accessories, etc. Most baby items are used for such a short period of time it saves money if everyone shares. You could also set up a lend table where people could write down things like baby swings, infant seats, etc., that they are not using right now, but want returned. If you want to make it game-like, set it up like an auction, giving poker chips out at the door based on the value of the items being donated.

228

Thanksgiving Box

Materials
Shoebox
Decorations: paint, paper, markers, etc.

Decorate the shoebox and cut a slit in the top large enough to fit folded pieces of paper. Put a small pile of scrap paper and a pen next to the box. Write anything that happens that you are thankful for and place the notes in the box. All family members can contribute to the box. You can even write things for baby, like, "I'm thankful I can finally eat solid food." On Thanksgiving or another celebrated day, read all the slips in the box. Remember to write in the little daily things that occur. They will bring a smile to everyone's face as they rekindle memories.

Winter Picnic

Pick a day in the middle of winter when everyone in the family is sick of staying indoors and make a summer-style picnic. Gather the soft balls that can be thrown in the house without destroying everything, and get out favorite games. Lay out a large tablecloth on the family room floor and get ready to munch. While lunching, share favorite summer memories. Baby is sure to love this style of eating, since all his or her favorite people are at eye level. It may be so much fun that a weekly picnic could be planned!

230

Sing Along

231

Materials
Cassette tape of music baby has heard
many times
Words to a few of the songs written down
for family members
Homemade instruments: drum, tambourine,
or bells

Make sure baby is on the same level as
everyone else, either in a high chair while
everyone sits around the table, or all sitting
on the floor. Put the tape on and everyone
sing softly with the tape. As baby gets used
to it and starts to smile, add instruments,
arm movements, and clapping hands. Baby
will feel the joy and will be thrilled to be
included in the group fun.

Christmas Morning

Here's a tradition to start on baby's first Christmas, since, as baby grows older, it may mean you sleep until 7 a.m. instead of 5 a.m. on Christmas morning! Fill baby's stocking full of small presents that can be looked at and played with without your assistance. Baby will wake up, see the stocking, and be delightfully surprised. You may want to make this a birthday tradition as well. Surprises are fun for you and baby and can create wonderful memories!

232

The Way We Were

233

Invite friends over who have children. Ask each person to bring ten pictures of themselves before they had children. One or two couples at a time get to play the Newlywed Game. Using the pictures to spark ideas, the audience creates ten questions. One partner goes out of the room while the other answers the questions. Then the out-of-room partner comes in and tries to guess how the other answered the questions. The couple that gets the most questions correct wins. Here are a few hard to remember funny questions: When and where was your first kiss? What color is your wife's bathrobe? Where is the most unusual place you have made love? Who was your best friend in grade school? What is your favorite thing to do? What would be your ideal date? Be creative in creating the questions and have fun!

Spring Is Here

Prepare box breakfasts on a Friday or Saturday night. They might include small cartons of milk or juice, muffins, hard-boiled eggs, or yogurt. Include a special note to each person. Before everyone gets up, hide the breakfasts outside in the garden. Leave a note on the kitchen table letting everyone know they must search for their breakfasts. If children cannot read yet, wait for them to walk into the kitchen, then tell everyone at the same time to begin the search. Also hide packets of flower and vegetable seeds or bulbs to be found and planted. Set up an outdoor table and eat breakfast together. After breakfast, find the seeds and bulbs to plant in the garden together.

234

Husbands as Servants

OK Dad, it's time for you to plan a party your wife will love! Invite a few couples over, making sure the men involved talk beforehand about the theme. Make a list of ten things the men decide together that their wives would like: a foot or back massage, a walk in the garden, a dance, a poem recited, etc. Put each idea in a hat and let the women pick from the hat. Their husband has to do what is on the piece of paper. Of course the men make dinner and clean up as well, so the women can sit back, relax, and talk. It's worth it guys, she'll always remember it!

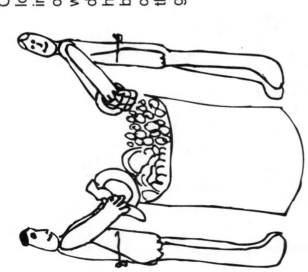

235

Family Growth

Point of View

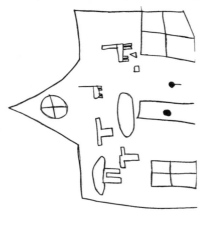

Do you find yourself feeling your home isn't what it used to be, that things look messy and toys are everywhere? Well, there is no known way to eliminate the disorder, so the best thing to do is change your point of view! Sit down and talk as a couple about how the changes affect each of you. If possible, provide a play area for your child where toys can be put away, and put up objects that could hurt baby or that baby could break. Most babies seem to have toys occupying space in every room of the house. If both of you can accept this as something that will pass, you will both be happier and your expectations will not bring unnecessary pressure.

Wit & Wisdom: When you get into a tight place and everything goes against you, till it seems you could not hold on a minute longer, never give up then, for that is just the place and time that the tide will turn.

—Harriet Beecher Stowe

236

Family Journal

Find a place to put a large blank book so family members know where it is and will be encouraged to write regularly. This blank book can be used as a daily diary or as a special events book. Children too young to write can dictate stories and draw handprints. Those too young to talk can be represented by weekly pictures with descriptions of new things they can do. The book can contain all aspects of family life. Visitors can write their names and a little about their visits, children can write their Christmas or birthday wish lists, baby's first words can be recorded, pictures drawn at school can be glued in. We guarantee this book will be a sought-after treasure in years to come.

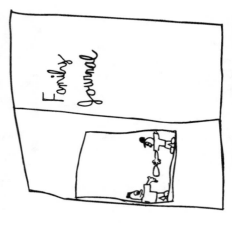

237

Perfect Imperfection

Everyone needs to feel pleased with themselves and family members can help each other by pointing out good effort. Don't make the mistake of waiting for someone to do something perfectly before you say something positive. Today, tell your child or spouse something you think they do well, something you think you can both be proud of. Take a minute to think of all the things you do in your own life. Can you feel satisfied with a few things in your life without expecting perfection? Recognizing your own perfect imperfection and calling attention to the positive things family members do will increase everyone's feelings of self-esteem. Do this for two weeks without missing a day and see what changes you notice.

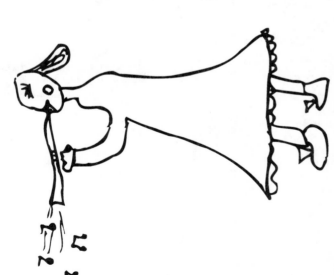

238

Family Postcards

On baby's birth announcement or the next time you mail out holiday cards to family and friends, ask each family to send baby a postcard of their hometown with a special note written especially for baby. Put the postcards in a photo book for baby to look at and save. When the postcards come in, talk to baby about who sent them. Keep up baby's postcard book by sending and encouraging others to send postcards from their home or travels.

239

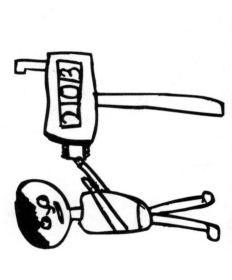

Teaching Compassion

If you want to teach baby compassion, you have to model and teach it. If they watch you reaching out to help people, they will grow up doing the same. Here are a few ideas:

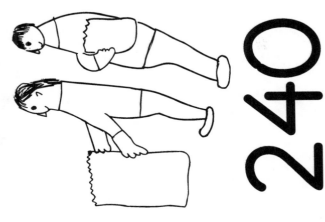

- Let someone in the grocery store go ahead of you if they have less or seem to be in a hurry.
- Offer to carry someone's groceries out to their car.
- Help another parent who might be struggling with their kids on a plane or at a restaurant. (They may need a trip to the bathroom but have nobody to hold the baby.)
- Make dinner for a sick neighbor.
- Say hello and smile at people you pass by!
- Give food to a beggar on the street.
- Make only positive comments about people who are different from you.

Who Are You?

Kids of all ages need insight into you as a person. Sometimes parents are so busy working and taking care of the family that the children don't see the person who is inside the mother or father. Start now by sharing things that happen at work, good jokes you may have heard, funny stories, a good book or movie, people you meet, etc. Even if baby doesn't quite understand, it's a good pattern to develop and continue as baby grows.

241

Wit & Wisdom: I once read an article which recommended that instead of asking a million questions about your child's day when you pick them up from school, tell them something interesting or strange that happened to you. The conversation will engage everyone, and children will not feel interrogated or pressured to answer the usual questions. The method works, try it!

—*Nina Nielsen, Woodside, CA*

Do Nothing Day

Pick one day a month as a "do nothing day." Everyone is free from chores, sort of like a sick day without being sick. Rooms stay messy while everyone does exactly what they want. This might be a good night to plan dinner out as a family. Of course with babies some things have to be done, but eliminate as many of the other chores as possible. This is a great family tradition, and as children grow it encourages them to be more responsible for themselves on these special days.

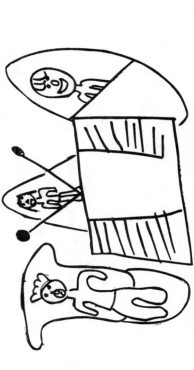

242

Love Letter

243

With a new baby around, you and your spouse may have less time to spend alone together and less time to express your love for each other. So, don't wait for Valentine's Day to write a love letter to your spouse. Most of us feel silly writing love letters, but we all blush upon receiving one as we proceed to read the letter over and over! Letters are one of the best ways to say something you might be too embarrassed to say in person. For a little fun, add a few gift vouchers, made and performed by you, for things you know your partner likes. Be creative and remember to keep the romance alive!

Wit & Wisdom: If possible, take an overnight together in a nearby town or the same city. Stay in an inexpensive motel, see a movie, walk, hike, and relax. One and a half days will seem like three! Do it every couple of months, it will keep you "in synch" with each other.

—*Laura Sullivan, Golden Valley, MN*

New Traditions

A tradition is something your family repeatedly does together that everyone likes and wants to have as a "traditional" part of family life. The shared meaning and memories that traditions create brings family members closer to each other. New traditions can be started today in your family. Take some time to think about traditions that were in your original families. Make a list of traditions that you both agree you would like to pass down, and talk about new possibilities. Here are a few ideas:

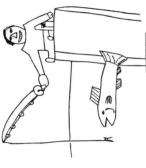

- Game night
- Letter writing night
- Family dinner together one night per week
- Family meetings
- Sharing time after dinner
- Family field trip one Saturday per month
- Bedtime stories

Be as open-minded as you can and create a long list. Decide on one, give it a try, and if everyone likes it, do it again. If it's meant to become a tradition, family members will want to experience it again and again.

244

Memory Lane

Set aside some time to share memories together as a couple or as a family. Watch home videos and look through picture albums. Let your children tell you what they remember, then adults can fill in forgotten details. Moments we set aside to share common experiences strengthen bonds and create a sense of security for everyone.

Wit & Wisdom: Please name and date baby pictures. Believe it or not, memories do fade and when there is more than one child, sometimes confusion arises.

—Sandy Welsh, Galesburg, IL

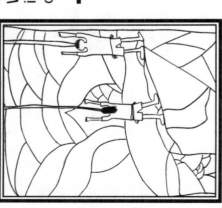

245

Surprise

Surprises are so much fun to give—and to receive! Pick a day and time to surprise your mate. Here are a few suggestions:

- Hire a baby-sitter and take your mate out for a meal, movie, dancing, etc.
- Buy a small gift for no reason and put it on their pillow.
- Invite a friend over you know they would like to see, buy a special dessert for the visit, then leave them alone to talk.
- Make reservations at a hotel for the night, and leave a message for him or her to meet you.

Be creative! You know what your partner likes, so take the time to do it now and then and you'll both reap the benefits.

246

Thirty Minute Talk

The following exercise is guaranteed to improve your marriage, no matter how good it already is! It's amazing how much you will each look forward to this special time. Pick a time that is convenient for both of you which can be kept like an appointment each day. Set a timer for fifteen minutes and one of you begin to talk about whatever you want: your day, problems, work, your relationship, kids, a hobby, etc. The other person just listens. Switch after fifteen minutes so you each get fifteen minutes of uninterrupted talk.

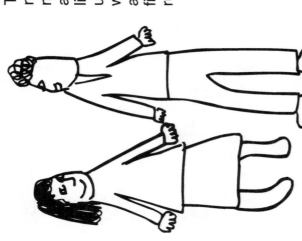

Video Moments

Rent or borrow a video camera if you don't own one, and recruit an assistant to help you if you can. Decide what everyday activities you will record and find your props. Record a day in the life of your baby. Start the video early in the morning while baby is still sleeping, catch baby waking up, getting dressed, eating, playing, riding in the car, walking, or in the stroller. Record baby with siblings or friends and follow baby all day through bathtime until bedtime. Make sure you have someone to help so you can be recorded with baby! Do a video day every six months, adding to the same tape each time. Baby will enjoy watching this as they grow, and will be thrilled with it when they have children of their own!

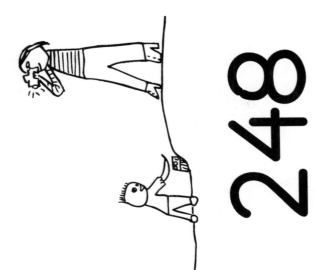

248

Play Date

Sometimes as adults we forget how to play with each other. So much time is spent working, dealing with kids, discussing finances, and coping with life, there seems to be no time to play. Play is important. It keeps the spirit alive and it reminds us that life is fun. Decide on a time when you will let yourself play. Go someplace with your partner like a bowling alley, a golf course, a swimming pool, etc. Laugh together, be silly, imagine, and dream. Declare one night a week as game night at home; play cards, charades, or a board game everyone likes. Make having fun together a priority!

249

Play Hooky

Every once in awhile it rejuvenates the soul to play hooky. Call in sick to work or school and take the day to do something fun. When everyone else is working or at school, places that are usually packed are relatively empty. Invite grandparents to join in the fun.

Wit & Wisdom: I remember one morning my mother came into my room before school and asked me if I would rather go skiing with her instead of going to school. I felt so lucky, like it was my birthday or some special event. That memory stuck in my head and taught me more about life than a year of school.

—Yvonne A., Ann Arbor, MI

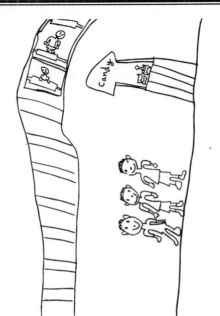

250

Mother's Time

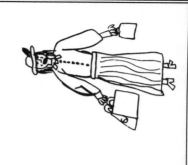

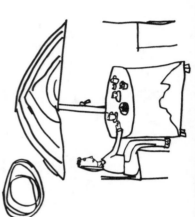

What Is a Mother?

A mother is not replaceable in a child's heart. If you are holding this book in hand, there is a child in your life that you are mothering in some way. Have you ever taken the time to think about what an amazing job it is to be a mother? What is a mother to you? What did you receive from your mother that you want to pass on to your child? What did you wish you received? What are your dreams as a mother? Who are you to your child? Take 15 minutes to think and write about what it means to be a mother.

251

Tea for You

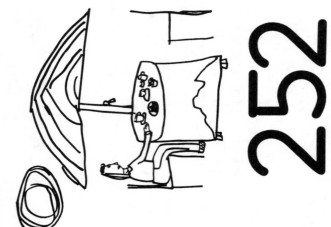

Take time out for a few minutes of calm at least once a day. Make a cup of hot tea or coffee, take the phone off the hook, and just relax. Read a good magazine article or shut your eyes and daydream. Don't get up for at least 15 minutes, no matter what!

Wit & Wisdom: Someone gave me this quote from William Lyons Phelps that made a lot of sense to me: "Real happiness is not dependent on external things. The pond is fed from within. The kind of happiness that stays with you is the happiness that springs from inward thoughts and emotions."

—*Liliana Kochanek, Hendersonville, TN*

252

Surrender Control

In order for mother to have some time to herself, other people have to help. That means things may not be done exactly as mother wishes. Clothes may be folded and put in the wrong piles, the dishwasher might be loaded out of order, your mail might be mixed up, etc. Practice surrendering control. For one week, let your husband, mother, baby-sitter, etc., do things their way. Just sit back and enjoy the fact that YOU are not doing them.

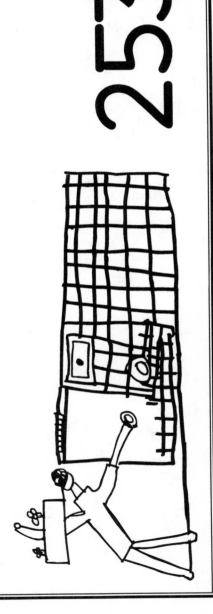

253

Vision Poster

Materials
Old magazines
Scissors
Glue
Poster board

Take an evening to make a poster with pictures that represent things you want in your life. Look through magazines to find pictures that represent your "vision" of what you want your life to be: a couple embracing could mean a close relationship, a picture of a baby might mean another child, etc. Hang this poster where you can see it often: a closet or bathroom door works well. It's inspiring to focus on possibilities.

Wit & Wisdom: I read a quote from Theodore Roosevelt a few years ago and it has become my motto. "Whenever you are asked if you can do a job, tell 'em, 'Certainly I can!' Then get busy and find out how to do it."

—*Annie H., Dallas, TX*

254

Write It Now

Materials
All sorts of postcards
Blank note cards
Calendar book
Assorted pretty stamps
Basket or box

Postcards are so quick to write if you have everything in one place ready to go! You may think if you don't have time to sit and write a long letter, filling friends and family in on all the details of life, that you shouldn't write at all. It's not true. Everyone enjoys getting mail of any kind, so take a little time each week to keep in touch. Write on a blank calendar who you wrote to and when. It will remind you of all the people you care about, and who care about you.

Role Models

In olden days, older and wiser women in the family passed down skill and knowledge to new mothers. Today, extended families live farther apart, so new mothers are left to fend for themselves without the timeless advice of elders. Yet role models do exist in your community and within your circle of friends. Take a few minutes and think about the women you know that you admire for some reason. Would you feel comfortable asking them for advice or discussing your fears? It is important to reach out and be open to learning new skills. Tell someone you admire that you see them as a role model, and ask them if they would mind you asking their advice and support on a regular basis. There is no greater compliment for the woman you ask, so be brave and reach out!

Wit & Wisdom: If you see a friend in need, don't ask them what you can do for them, think up something and just do it!

—Bonnie T., Buffalo, NY

256

Fun Time

It is important for a mom to find time to do fun things for herself, otherwise, she can get worn out, and lose enthusiasm for life. Forget that you barely have time to brush your teeth and make a list of things that are fun for you. Things as simple as a 30 minute, uninterrupted phone call count when you're a mom! Make sure the list includes as many fun things as you can think of. Post the list somewhere that you will see it every day. Here is the hard part: allow yourself to do one item off the list every day without feeling any guilt that you should be doing something else. Even as children grow, it is important for them to see that mom values herself. It's good for your health and theirs. Your children will respect you for respecting yourself, as well as learning to value their own needs by modeling your behavior. Everyone wins, so have some fun!

Jazz Clean

Each day, some time is spent tidying up the house, even if you don't want to. So why not make it a fun hour of exercise and music. Put on your tennis shoes and workout gear. When you bend to pick something up, do twenty plies. Run from room to room, or do jumping jacks and leg kicks. While on the floor, do a few sit ups and push ups. Fold clothes while doing standing leg lifts. Playing your favorite music loudly, just move, dance, and breathe. Set an amount of time you want to devote to cleaning and don't go over it. Save the rest to do tomorrow!

Learn It Together

Put together a list of other mothers you know: from labor classes, the neighborhood, church, etc. Decide on something you would like to learn, such as first-aid, baby massage, beauty makeover, yoga, etc. Send invitations or print up fliers to invite other mothers to the event. Hire someone to come and teach the class. If the cost is more than you want to spend, state on the invitation that there will be a charge. Don't worry, nobody will mind chipping in, and besides, if it's a subject that interests you, chances are other mothers will enjoy learning it too. You may want to hire a baby-sitter for everyone to share. On the day of the event, serve coffee, tea, or juice and a simple food, like muffins, bagels, or cookies. If it goes well, maybe you could discuss doing another one. Get someone else to volunteer to organize the next event. Who knows, this may become a monthly meeting.

Buy Flowers

Flowers make a home feel alive, happy, and bright. They refresh the spirit! If you have flowers in your yard, pick them often, and if not, buy some from the farmers market once in a while. Even branches with pretty fall leaves will work if you are on a budget. Gaze at the flowers throughout the day, and pick off the dead buds and rearrange into appropriate vases during the week. Every effort made to make daily life special is an affirmation that you are important and worth spending time on.

Wit & Wisdom: When you have only two pennies left in the world, buy a loaf of bread with one, and a lily with the other.

—Chinese Proverb

260

Special Photo Album

Every time a roll of film is developed, there always seems to be one picture you stare at in awe. It captures your child, a favorite memory, or an unforgettable event so perfectly. Buy a beautiful picture album more decorative than the family's ordinary one. Put that special photo memory in it. You will never have to waste time rummaging through piles of pictures to find that special one. It may take ten years to fill it up, but in the end it will be your prized possession.

261

Time to Organize

With small children, life has to be simplified in order to survive! Start by committing one day each month to organizing some part of your life. Start with your closet. Try everything on to see what still fits. If you haven't worn something in a year, give it away. Try to pick two or three colors that your wardrobe revolves around. This makes dressing much easier, and saves money on accessories! So your closet doesn't look packed, box up seasonal clothes, adding scented soap to the box for freshness upon opening. Do this closet cleaning at least twice a year. To save time, buy your underwear and nylons two times a year. Shop from catalogues after baby is asleep. Look forward to organization day each month and don't feel guilty in between dates—you will get to it on schedule.

262

Fast Makeover

Moms need their makeup on and hair done in less than 15 minutes, am I right? It's worth putting a little extra effort and practice into getting a quick routine in place. If you're convincing yourself you don't care what you look like because no one will see you, you're wrong. You will see you, and that counts! If you look a mess, you'll most likely feel a mess. Even while wearing a sweatsuit, you can look put together. Go get a makeover and make sure to tell the makeup artist that you need one you can do in seven minutes. Bring your own makeup so you won't be tempted to buy everything they use. It's also a good idea to pick an easy hairstyle that can be completed in under ten minutes. You'll feel great about the new you!

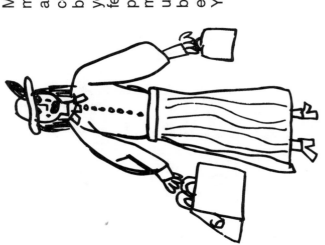

263

Weekend Escape

With or without your partner, you must get away from it all every so often. The word vacation comes from the Latin word *vacatio*, which means freedom, to be empty, or release from occupation. Take two days and stay in a hotel or country inn near where you live. Order room service, see a play, act as if you took a plane and traveled very far for a vacation. After just two days, you will return refreshed with new energy.

264

Dad's Time

Baby's World

If you're a dad who works every day, not having as much time as you would like to spend with a child, try this: spend at least 30 minutes with your baby doing nothing but being there. Follow baby no matter what he does—if he crawls, crawl along; if he babbles, babble back; if he wants to sing a song, clap along. What does the world look like at baby's eye level? The idea is for you to let the child direct you, and for you to step into the child's world. This is a great bonding experience to do with older children as well. In fact, if you do this once a week until they leave home, you have given your child an amazing gift...you paid attention!

What Is a Father?

Take a few minutes out of your day to think about your father: his strengths, weaknesses, the time you spent together, what he taught you about life, etc. What kind of father do you want to be? Write down your goals as a father. Who do you want to be to your child? What do you want to teach him or her? How do you plan to show your love and concern each day?

Wit & Wisdom: The presents my father most appreciated were the bookmarks I made for him out of the grandchildren's photographs. I simply laminated them.
—*Brennan T., Lake Tahoe, CA*

266

Another Dad

267

Make the effort to become friends with another man who also has a baby. Look around at work, at the gym, the park, or wherever you spend time. Dads need support too; life has changed, and you need to learn a new role. This friend you find will be going through similar changes in his life, so walk the path together. Plan trips together to the park, zoo, lake, etc. Talk about your babies and your feelings as new fathers.

Wit & Wisdom: Whenever I take my kids to events where we have seats, I pin their ticket stubs to their shirts so that if they get lost, the usher can bring them back.

—*Dennis P., Boulder, CO*

Mother and Wife

The woman in your life plays the roles of wife, mother, and lover. Take a few minutes to examine how you see her in each of these roles. Do you give encouragement and support her in each of these roles, or do you emphasize one role more than another? Do you make time for her in each of her roles? Do you tell her what you need from her in each of these roles? Take time today to tell her that you see her as all these women, and that you love every aspect of her.

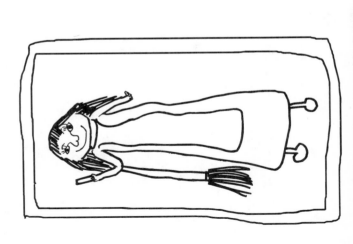

Reality to Fantasy

269

What would your life be like if you lived in a castle? What would you do if you were president? How would you feel if you were the world's best at something? What would you do with millions of dollars? Write down all of your thoughts. Visualizing yourself having great wealth, success, or happiness will bring a smile to your face. The point is that it's fun to dream, to step out of reality and into fantasy once in a while.

Wit & Wisdom: When I took my two toddlers to the beach, I always brought a small inflatable pool I would place near the water and fill with ocean water. The kids were close to the sand and waves, and could play in the pool water without my constant worry.

—Allan C., San Diego, CA

Dad Things

Some things dads just seem to do better than moms: things like wrestling, rolling in the leaves, fishing, galloping around the house, and washing the car. Make a mental list of the things you like to do with baby that mom doesn't really care to do. Make an extra effort to do these things with baby. Special time with dad is very important.

Wit & Wisdom: I love to hike with my infant son on my back. It always bothered me that I couldn't see his face, so I tied a lightweight mirror around my neck. Now I can pick up the mirror and smile at him whenever I want to.

—*Matt H., Orlando, FL*

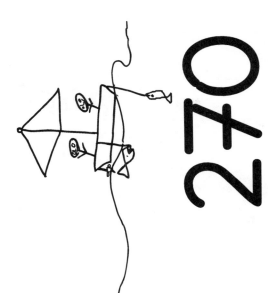

270

Who Are You?

Do you have hobbies or special interests? It is important that as baby grows he *really* knows you. What better way than to share with him things you like to do? Start early. When you pick out books at the library, pick them on subjects that interest you, then share your joy. When you go someplace special, bring baby along. Point out things you like. Make silly jokes. Talk about your work when you get home, telling baby what you do all day. Of course, you also have to reciprocate and express interest in baby's life!

271

Wit & Wisdom: Whenever I travel to a new city, I bring back a map of the area. I laminate the maps and use them as place mats. That way I can point to all the places I was and talk about what I did when I was gone on business.

—*Phil M., Sacramento, CA*

Box Forts, Tunnels, and Tents

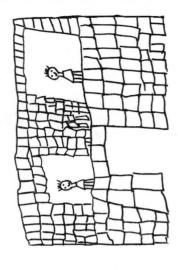

Materials
Lots of old boxes
Sheet or blanket
Rubber bands

Here's a fun all-day activity for inside or outside. So many exciting things can be done with old boxes and lots of imagination. Design a masterpiece: use boxes with a sheet over the top to make a tunnel, fasten the sheets to chair tops with the rubber bands and make tents, stack boxes high to make towers, or crawl inside boxes to hide. If baby gets tired of crawling in and out of boxes, she can crawl over and under dad, the man-made bridge and tunnel!

—Paul W., Nashville, TN

Wit & Wisdom: I keep several water-filled balloons in the freezer, just in case of a bump or bruise. Make sure to wrap it in a towel first.

Alone with Baby

Plan a block of time each week that you spend completely alone with baby. You can learn so much about each other and grow attached in ways that are impossible when mom is around. In this block of time, pay attention to baby and really be together, with no television on, no phones ringing, and no paper being read as baby watches you. A little time goes a long way!

Wit & Wisdom: When I need to wake up my daughter from a nap, I sit by her bed and start softly reading a favorite story. She wakes up happy and eager to listen.

—Stuart P., Denver, CO

273

Junk Mailman

As you sort through your mail and pay your bills, let baby sit beside you and open all of the junk mail. Babies love to rip paper (be careful of paper cuts). This will keep them occupied for as long as you need to go through your bills. You may even have time to read the paper! If baby is old enough, you can also pretend to be mail carriers going out to the mailbox, then delivering mail to people.

274

Shoebox Train

Materials
Old shoeboxes (5 or 6 of them)
String or twine

Babies love to pull things. Dad, this is your project since construction and sound effects are usually a specialty! String the shoeboxes together using an in and out sewing pattern so the boxes will pull in a straight line. Start at the last box and work forward, tying the end so baby has a handle to pull. Once the train is made, put a few of baby's small toys in it. If you have a train whistle, blow it. If not, you'll have to pretend you're the conductor by making all the appropriate sounds.

275

Talk About Feelings

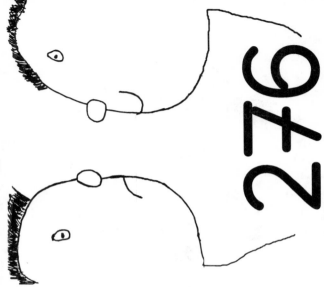

It's very important that you talk to your wife about how it feels to be a dad. In fact, it would be a good idea if you took the time to write your wife a letter telling her what your new role means to you. Tell her all your feelings, the good and the not so good. Tell her how much you appreciate the little daily jobs she does. Tell her what a good mother she is. Reassure her that she is still as sexy as before the baby. Tell her what you need. When children are young, along with positive feedback, open communication is what will help you survive. Encourage each other to open up and express yourselves.

Wit & Wisdom: I was afraid to give my first child a bath because she was so small and slippery in the water, so I put a pair of white cotton sports socks on my hands and she didn't feel so slippery.

—*Alex B., Stockton, CA*

Sex After Baby

Life with baby often means less of a sex life. Everyone is exhausted by bedtime! Nobody will disagree with you that it's hard work to keep the passion alive in your relationship, but there are ways. Here are a few:

- Have an affair with your wife. Write her a sexually explicit love letter, then give her a time and place to meet you.

- Accept your wife's new body after she has a child. It is difficult for her to go through her own bodily changes. She will feel sexier if you are positive and supportive.

- Make weekly dates for sex. Take turns setting the scene. It will give you both something to look forward to and depend on.

- Every woman loves a massage, and it will most likely lead to something else.

Siblings

You Are Great

Make sure your other children overhear you saying great things about them! So often when a new baby arrives the talk is all about baby, even though baby can't hear it or appreciate it. The older brother or sister is usually standing right there hearing all of the raving. So, tell a few of your friends and family the plan, which is to talk about your other children as well. Next time you are having tea or talking on the phone, talk about how much fun you have with them, what great things they are doing, and how lucky you are to have such great kids.

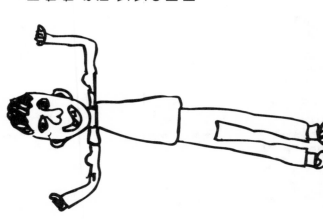

A Picture of Me

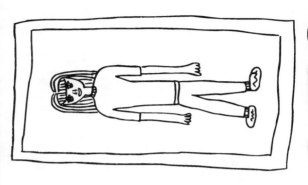

Materials
Picture of big brother or sister
Poster board
Markers
Stickers
Glue

Have the older child glue a picture of themselves to the poster board and decorate it however they would like. Write "Big Brother" or "Big Sister" on the board. Let the artist decide where in baby's room to hang their portrait. Make sure baby can see it often. Siblings can feel less important when they get less time and attention, especially if they have been the only child for a while. To help build an older child's self-esteem, include them in decisions about baby and repeatedly tell them how wonderful, important, and helpful they are. Frequent hugs are important too!

Child's Photo Album

Materials
4" by 6" photo album
Current family photos

Whenever you have pictures developed, make sure to have two copies made. Brothers and sisters like having their very own picture albums full of pictures of THEM, so make sure you don't just take pictures of baby. Each time you get a roll of film developed, let your child pick out a few pictures they want to add to their own album. This also gives them something to do while you are putting pictures in the family albums.

280

A Hero's Story

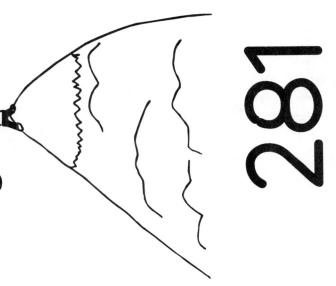

Spontaneously tell a story during a quiet time or at bedtime about baby's brother or sister. Build their self-esteem by bringing up all the things they do each day for you, for baby, at school, playing, etc. Make the sibling the hero in some way—someone baby and everyone else looks up to. Stories like this work well because everyone can listen at the same time, baby may be entertained, and big brothers and sisters feel very important. You may even want to tape record these stories, as children love to hear them over and over. Even if you have doubts about your storytelling ability, the kids will love it simply because you made it up!

Big Brother and Sister Shirts

Materials
Fabric pen
Fabric paint
Large sponge
White T-shirts
Large piece of cardboard to fit inside
T-shirt to stretch it out while being
painted

Write the words "I'm the Big Brother" or
"I'm the Big Sister" on the blank T-shirts
and let them dry. Using one color of fabric
paint at a time, pour a little fabric paint on
top of the sponge and rub it around. Rub
baby's foot on top of the sponge, then step
it onto the shirt. Repeat with the same
color for as many footprints as you like. Let
older siblings help direct the design.

Change the
color on the
sponge and
make prints in
other colors.

Note: Make a
shirt for baby
too that says,
"Everyone loves me," and let the older siblings put their handprints on it!

How I Feel

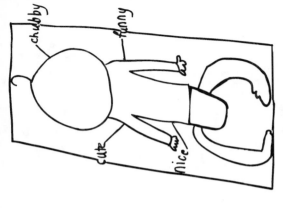

Materials
Sheet of butcher paper long enough to fit the tallest
    child's body outline
Crayons or markers

Have each child, including baby, lie on the sheet of butcher
paper individually. Take the marker or crayon and outline
each body. Have each sibling talk about how they feel about
baby, how baby has changed their lives for better or worse,
what they like and dislike about baby, and anything else you
can think of. Write these things inside the outline of the baby.
Be sure to let them know you understand all their feelings!
Then ask the siblings how they think baby feels about them
and write this inside their outline. It is important that every-
body in a family believes their feelings matter. New babies
change the makeup of your family, and talking about the
changes helps everyone!

Puppet Theater

Materials
Refrigerator box
Paint
Fabric for curtains

An old refrigerator box makes a perfect puppet theater. The adult needs to do the cutting out, but after that, let the kids decorate. They will be so proud of their theater design and will be thrilled to have baby and parents attend opening night! First, tape any top or bottom flaps closed to make the box more sturdy. Stand the box up vertically, then cut a two foot tall hole at the very top of the box on the side that would face the audience. This will be the stage. Then, cut a three foot tall hole on the opposite side bottom so the children can crawl in. Let the kids design the outside. Staple fabric to the stage top and tie it at each side for curtains.

284

Nature Collage

285

Materials
Flat items found in nature: leaves,
  flower petals, grass, feathers, etc.
Flat box lid
Glue
Paper

Have the older children point out to baby the kinds of
things to look for outside. Chances are baby will pull the
whole flower out, but that's OK; you can take the petals off
later. Put all the collected items on the flat box lid. The
adult or one of the siblings draws an outline of a butterfly,
animal, flower, etc. Make this outline large and simple. Put
glue directly onto the paper in small sections at a time.
Help baby place the nature collectibles on the glued sections. Sometimes it is best to drop a flower petal and see
where it lands. Once there are many leaves and petals on
the paper, put a paper towel on top and rub gently.

Homemade Picture Book

Materials
Old magazines
Scissors
Glue
Construction paper—plain or colored, or a
scrapbook with plain paper pages

Go through the magazine briefly with your older
child, showing them the kinds of pictures to cut out.
Look for things that baby might recognize: animals,
house, people, car, plants, etc. Cut out pictures and
glue them onto the paper or scrapbook. If your
older child wants to, they can write a descriptive
word underneath each picture. It's also fun to put
the pictures in some sort of order that tells a story.
Give the self-made picture book to baby. This could
be a special book that only the older brother or sister would be allowed to read or look at with baby.

Handprint Cookies

Materials
Cookie dough
Decorative frosting
Blunt knife

Cookie Dough Recipe:
1/2 cup brown sugar
1/2 cup butter
1 teaspoon vanilla
2 eggs
1/2 teaspoon salt

2 1/2 cups
    unbleached flour
2 teaspoons
    baking powder

Directions: Cream sugar, butter, vanilla, and eggs. Mix in flour, baking powder, and salt. Chill dough for 3 hours. Preheat oven to 375°F (190°C). Roll dough out on floured surface. Cut with shaped cookie cutters. Bake 7 to 10 minutes. Yield: 24 cookies.

Roll dough out to about 1/4" thickness, then put the child's hand on top of the dough and cut around the outside. Make a few cookies for each child. If you would rather make small cookies, just use a thumb print. Put them on a greased cookie sheet and bake. When cool, let children decorate the cookies. Babies love to feel soft squishy things, so let them play with the dough, and help to roll it out. Then watch the fun as everyone decorates.

287

Scavenger Hunt

288

Materials
Scavenger hunt items: cotton ball, aluminum foil, emery board, velvet, cork, rock, fake or real fur, wool, leaf, bark, flower

Large piece of cardboard
Glue

Give the older children a list of all the items they have to find. You may want to make a game out of it by setting a time limit and racing against time, or each other, to collect all the items. Once the items are collected, have the children glue them to the cardboard. Once the glue has dried, have big brother or sister take baby's hand and rub it over one item at a time on the board. The older child should say as much as they can think of about each item, for example, "the leaf is green, it is smooth, it grows on trees, some leaves fall to the ground in autumn, etc." This can be a great opportunity for the older sibling to feel their importance as baby's teacher.

Ring of Love

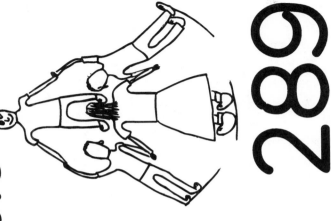

Materials
Your bodies, voices, and imagination
A room of any size

Move any pieces of furniture, toys, clothes, etc., out of the way so that you can hold hands and walk around in a circle (like ring around the rosie). The object of this activity is to have fun and at the same time give your child positive reinforcement. Hold hands and walk in a circle, first marching, then hopping, skipping, and running. Reverse direction often. As you do this, think of positive statements you could make, like, "We are nice and we can share," or "We love each other and we listen."

Layered Bottle Art

Materials
Decorative glass container
Dried goods: cereal, beans, grains, nuts, herbs

Set the glass container on a counter in the kitchen. Collect cereal, dried beans, macaroni, nuts, herbs, etc., and begin to put them into the glass container in layers. In no time at all you will have a decorative bottle of layered dried goods to place on a kitchen shelf. An older sibling could be in charge of directing the design and giving instructions as little fingers place the beans one at a time into the bottle.

Note: This must be closely supervised since it involves small things that baby could choke on.

290

Food Fair

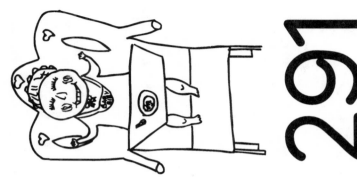

291

Materials
Assorted soft foods: finger food appropriate for
   baby, applesauce, pudding, etc.
Plate
Bowls
High chair

Prepare yourself, baby, and older siblings for food
tasting and exploration. Have all foods at hand
and ready to be eaten before starting. Place on
baby's tray one type of food at a time and do the
same on the other plates. Allow baby freedom to
explore the taste, smell, texture, size, sound, and
temperature of each. Then give baby an opportunity to compare foods by putting two or three different foods on his or her tray. Big brother or sister might have some suggestions of their own.
Enjoy what your little chefs create!

Where's Your Bottle?

Here is a game an older sibling can play anytime and anyplace with baby. Simply ask a question or suggest an action, then work together to do what was asked. For example: "Where's your blanket? Let's go watch the gardener! What's in the toy box? Let's practice talking on the phone; Let's go find the dog; Where is the garage?" Change the requests depending on baby's abilities. Of course, half the fun is for the older sibling to know the answer and help baby to find his or her way. Make sure baby doesn't just point to the object or action mentioned—the children have to go together to find it.

292

Grandparenting

What Do You Need?

It's easy to remember how it felt to be exhausted from the work of parenting. When you go to visit your child, remember that you are walking into their parenting life and they may do things differently than you did. Ask a few simple questions when you arrive so that you feel comfortable.

• The first and most important is "What can I do each day that will help you?" (For example, take baby for a few hours each morning.)

• Could you write down the daily schedule?

• Is there a special way you do certain things, like the dishes, laundry, vacuuming, playing with baby, etc.?

• Is there anything I should not do with baby?

• What does baby like?

• What are baby's habits and developmental level right now?

• Think of any other questions that you want to ask, and remember that open communication will make the visit more enjoyable!

Meet the Neighborhood

Before the grandkids arrive, make a point to look for children in your neighborhood that look about the same age. Introduce yourself to their parents and tell them your grandchildren will be arriving soon for a visit. You might even be able to borrow toys, bikes, dolls, cribs, strollers, or car seats. Also, ask them to recommend a pediatrician and a baby-sitter so you will be prepared in case of emergency.

294

Food for Thought

It's funny how parents just don't seem to feed kids things they like, but at Grandma and Grandpa's house the food is great! Instead of shopping before the grandkids arrive, wait until they are with you to go shopping. Plan the menu together, then go to the store to pick out a few things. Let each child pick out a box of cereal to be their own and write their name on the box with a thick marker. Even with baby food, mom might have changed the brand since the last visit. So, at the very least, make sure to inquire beforehand what food to purchase. It's not fun to be stuck with a lot of food that the kids won't eat!

GROCERY

potatoe chips

295

Establish a Play Area

If grandchildren will be spending time at your house, there are a few things you can do that will make visits more fun for everyone:

1. Start a separate cabinet where craft supplies are stored. The list should include crayons, paper, playdough (or see the Clay and Playdough chapter and make some), finger paint, old boxes, wrapping paper scraps, scissors, glue stick, old magazines, old socks, felt, etc.

2. Start a dress-up box. As you do your yearly closet cleaning, save the old jackets, dresses, high heeled shoes, jewelry, hats, ties, etc. Consider cutting the dress bottoms and coat arms to a reasonable length for the grandchildren.

3. Try to clean an area and designate it as a play area. Even a small area will do. This way there will be no excuse for having toys all over the house! Buy a cheap wall mirror and hang it up in this area, then watch the children find a million uses for it.

4. For inexpensive and instant room decorations the children will love, take a few photos of the kids and blow them up to poster size. Then, buy cheap plastic poster frames and hang them in the room where the children sleep.

296

Baby's Memories

Start a journal for baby. Include anything you would like. It's fun to do a daily log of the things you do together on the days you spend with each other. In between visits you might include drawings sent from the child or letters sent by their parents. You may want to write poems, describe the daily world news, or relate similar experiences from your own life. Whatever you decide to write will be cherished, and will be a different point of view from what their parents would write!

Wit & Wisdom: If a toddler is having trouble with their first steps, place a clothespin in each hand and this will steady them, since it feels like adult fingers.

—Nancy Maley, Shorewood, MN

297

Excursions

Investigate what is going on for the children in your area. A good resource is the local parenting newspaper, which is usually free and available wherever you find services that cater to children, or call the local library and ask them. Look for live children's theaters, children's museums, farm visits, etc. Plan a few things to do in advance and schedule the week accordingly. It's amazing how much easier life goes when you have a plan!

Traditions

Decide on special traditions you want to pass on to your grandchildren. Make them traditions they may only do with you, like nature walks, nighttime bonfires, special meal menus, afternoon tea, a song at bedtime, etc. Think of the traditions in your family, pass on old traditions, or make up new ones. The important thing is to give the children things they can count on each time they are with you, as it makes them feel secure and special.

Wit & Wisdom: Sometimes when a baby is fussy and cross, I have found these secret words can work miracles. The words have been passed down from one generation to the next. Don't laugh, but the magic words are "tootie... tootie..." Hold the baby tightly and whisper "tootie... tootie..." over and over again in a low voice close to their ear. You will be surprised how soothing this is to them.

—Suzanne Roberts, Indianapolis, IN

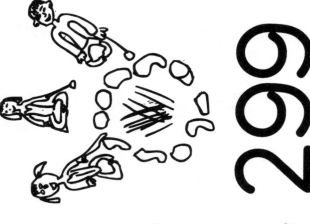

299

Photo Opportunity

Take many photographs of your grandbaby. Go through an entire day cataloging the simplest things, like waking up, eating breakfast, taking a walk, bath time, playing, etc. Make sure you are in some, if not all of the pictures. When you develop the film, make two prints—one for you and one for baby. Take the pictures and put them in a small picture album that baby can carry around. Write stick-on notes beneath the photos so that when you are not around someone else can read them to baby as a reminder of your days together. Put the second set of prints in an album for yourself, never to be touched by gooey hands!

300

Individual Attention

When visiting more than one grandchild at a time, make sure to spend individual time with each child. Children notice how much attention baby gets, so make an extra special effort with the older sibling to assure them of their continued place in your heart! A perfect time for you to create a special space for the older child is when Mom is nursing. Do a project, read a story, make up a puppet show, hug each other, go for a walk. Most importantly, pay attention to what the child says to you and listen intently. Make sure to get some time alone to hold and bond with baby too.

Wit & Wisdom: Try to treat identical twins as the individuals they are, e.g., try to give them some individual attention, don't always dress them alike, and give them names that don't sound alike.

—*Laura Sullivan, Golden Valley, MN*

301

Life on Tape

There is so much communicated in a voice. Whether you are an old or a young grandparent, you won't be alive forever, so start recording your life story on tape now. It will be a gift your grandchild may not even hear until they are ten years or older, but they will cherish it. Tell parts of your life intertwined with their lives, things you do together, impressions of their personality, your feelings and thoughts, the world's differences now from when you were a child, their parents' life adventures, etc. There doesn't have to be any pre-planned narration, just talk. Make a few notes to yourself about what areas were mentioned so you won't repeat yourself over the years. Add to your tapes at least once a month.

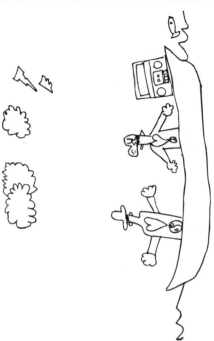

302

Plant a Garden

Plant a small garden together at your house or theirs! Simple vegetables like carrots, cucumbers, tomatoes, sunflowers, and pumpkins grow fast. Draw pictures of what you expect to grow and glue them to thick popsicle sticks. Push the sticks into the ground near the seeds. It might be fun to go to the store, get some grown vegetables like the ones you planted, and make something with them. If the grandchildren will not be visiting when the vegetables arrive, take pictures and send them with a little story about you caring for the garden!

303

Special Books

304

Do you remember any of the books that were read to you as a child? Do you remember the special books you read to your children? Start reading those books to your grandchild. Tell them how you used to read them to their mom or dad; tell them little things you remember, like how their dad loved this character, or was afraid of that one, or that their mother started dressing her stuffed animals just like the heroine. Even newborns like hearing the singsong of stories. Pass a part of yourself on and tape the stories so they can be played when you are not with them!

Picture Frame

Buy one of those large picture frames that has fifteen or twenty small picture spaces. In the spaces, put old pictures of the child's parents at similar ages. You may have fun posing baby in similar positions, then taking pictures of them to be added to the frame near the ones of their parents. Children like to see a resemblance between themselves and their parents. They also find it funny, and a bit hard to believe, that their parents were ever children!

Wit & Wisdom: Get a subscription to a national parenting magazine and read the articles. There are so many new ideas out, and so much information to help a parent, that were not around when you were raising your children.

—*Ruth G., Bridgeport, CT*

305

Grandma's Jewelry Box

Take some time on a rainy afternoon to pull out your old jewelry box (if you don't have one, visit the local thrift store). That big chunky costume jewelry that is no longer in style will light up your grandchild's eyes. Tell them stories about the events like weddings and parties you wore that jewelry to. If you have old pictures, pull those out too. Let the children try things on and look in the mirror. Don't give them all the jewelry at once; it's more fun for them to look forward to the surprises in Grandma's jewelry box.

Lullaby Lane

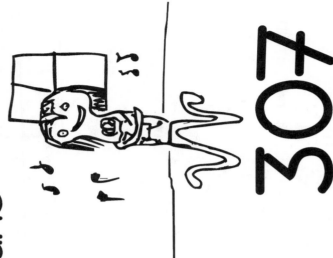

307

Sing lullabies that you remember to grand-baby. If you can't remember any, make one up so it can be passed on. Sing this lullaby every time you hold your grandba-by; other times simply hum the melody. Baby will begin to recognize this song and feel soothed when they hear it. If you live far away, make a tape of yourself singing a few songs, saying poems or rhymes, or reading stories.

Wit & Wisdom: When rocking or holding a baby, hold them tightly against your body. Do not flop them around from one position to another. Babies need a secure, warm feeling when they are being held.

—Suzanne Roberts, Indianapolis, IN

On the Go

ZOO

GROCERY

Travel Tips

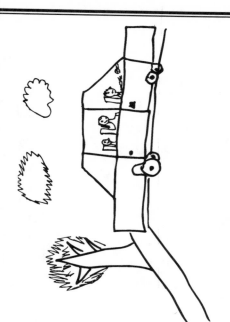

Taking trips with baby can be difficult, so here are a few ideas to make the trip more fun!

- Stop at least once every two hours, get out, walk around, and have a snack.
- Wrap many small presents and treats individually, then put them into a big bag and let baby pick one out every so often.
- Require a five to ten minute silent period every hour for the driver's peace of mind.
- Take turns singing songs or sing together.
- Make up stories about things you see along the way.
- Bring a hand puppet so when baby starts crying you can pop it over the seat and entertain.
- Invest in a few story and song cassettes to play in the car stereo as you go.

308

Where to Go

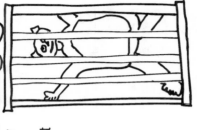

Here is a list of fun places to go with baby. If you are not sure what is available in your area, look for a local parenting paper. Many community recreation centers may also be able to help. The local library is also a great source for finding out about things.

you find interesting. Take baby places where they can get a hands-on experience. If you are at a performance of some sort, make sure to sit near an exit, as baby may get bored halfway through. Make sure to pack treats. Good luck!

Children's concerts
  or plays
Children's museums
Fire station
Local stores
Flower shows
Home shows
Circus
Parks
Television station

Fairs, exhibitions, or
  theme parks
Zoo or farm
Police station
Bakery, dairy
Boating shows
Major sporting events
Ice shows
Art museums

The list is endless. Remember, everything is new to baby, so point out things to them that

Restaurant Tips

If you're going to a restaurant with baby, remember:

- Go when the restaurant is not busy.
- Make sure that baby is hungry.
- If food is taking too long, tell your server you will be outside playing with your child, and ask if they could call you when the food arrives.
- Get crackers or bread and ask if they have crayons and paper.
- Pick restaurants that are set up for children with kid's menus, high chairs, etc.
- As soon as the child gets restless, order dessert or ice cream.
- You will probably not get dessert or coffee yourself, so save that for a time you're out without baby.

Don't forget to praise baby for all good behavior!

Napkin Art

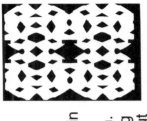

Materials
Paper napkins
Scissors

Make a point of carrying around a small scissors in your purse or in baby's bag. While sitting and waiting at a restaurant, pull the scissors out and make fascinating works of art out of napkins. Baby will be mesmerized watching you snipping away and unravelling a beautiful snowflake or people chain. Here's how you do it:

Snowflake: Fold napkin in half two times. Cut triangular and circular notches out of the edges all along the square. Fold the square in half and cut a few notches in the middle. Try this once and you'll see you can basically cut anywhere and a beautiful snowflake will still emerge. Open up the square and see what you get.

People Chain: Open napkin up, then fold at least three times in the same direction. Draw half a person, making sure to have the arm go out to the joined edge. Cut around the drawing and open it up, and you will have a chain of people holding hands.

311

Grocery Store Game

Take baby to the grocery store to explore, not to buy. Put baby in a shopping cart as you talk about how exciting the store is. Tell them about all the new things they will see and feel. Start wheeling the grocery cart up and down the aisles. If you see baby looking at or reaching for something, hand it to them as you continue to hold it with them. Rub the container against baby's hand and talk about the following things: shape, color, what is in it, whether it feels cold, hot, rough, or smooth. If you plan on buying anything, it might be fun to taste test as well. Go through the store letting baby investigate everything until baby loses interest.

Wit & Wisdom: Put prepared Jello in an empty baby food jar and freeze it. Take it in baby's bag in the morning and by lunch it will be ready to eat.

—*Kelly Tucker, San Mateo, CA*

GROCERY

312

Bring a Shoe

Materials
Old shoes with laces

Instead of giving away all your old shoes, save a few for baby's entertainment. Shoes are a great distraction while waiting someplace where quiet play is necessary. Make sure the shoelaces have plastic tips. Baby will most likely take the shoelaces out and you will have to relace them. It's fun to watch baby try to figure out what to do with the shoe and laces!

Wit & Wisdom: We often went to church with our children when they were babies. A soft, quiet baby shoe with shoelaces provided a task for busy hands as they laced and often relaced the shoe (depending on the length of homily!).

—*Joan Friske, St. Paul, MN*

313

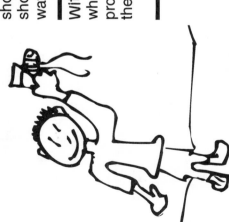

Spyglass Necklace

Materials
Cardboard toilet paper tubes
Different colors of cellophane
Rubber bands
Yarn or string

Cut the cellophane into four to five inch squares. Wrap cellophane over the end of one of the tubes and secure it with a rubber band. Carry one of these tubes in baby's bag to pull out in restaurants, stores, etc. Baby will enjoy looking at the surroundings and watching them turn different colors. Make many of these tubes of different colors and string them together to hang in the car or from the stroller. Baby

will be entertained while riding. Just make sure baby doesn't walk and look at the same time!

314

Touch Adventure

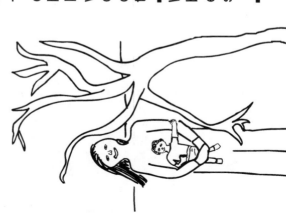

This activity can be done wherever you are with baby: inside, outside, in the car, at stores, in restaurants, etc. Take baby's hand and place it on an object. Name and describe the object. Don't worry if baby pulls away from the object, some babies want to look at an object for a while before touching it. Use colorful adjectives when describing the object. When baby gets older, make a guessing game out of it by closing your eyes and trying to guess what is being touched.

Wit & Wisdom: To keep baby's bottle cool on a hot day, fill a bottle with a few ounces of water, cap it, and put it in the freezer. Add the juice or water before you go out and the bottle will stay cool as the ice inside it melts.

—Amanda P., Aspen, CO

315

Out and About

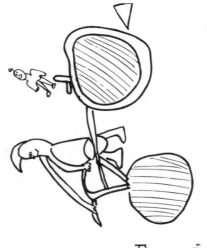

316

Materials
Car   Backpack
Bike   Blanket
Stroller

Take baby out of the house and go anywhere that there are sounds to be heard. Call baby's attention to the different sounds you both hear and name them out loud. Take special notice of the quiet sounds around you. Sit or stand quietly together and as you hear a sound you have already named repeat itself, notice it again and watch baby smile. As baby gets older, louder sounds, like a train, airplane, or sporting event might be added, but in the beginning (0 to 6 months) loud sounds might scare baby.

Wit & Wisdom: If baby has become attached to some sort of blanket, cut a piece of it off to take on trips instead of dragging the whole thing everywhere you go.
—Peter W., Carson City, NV

I Spy

This might be a game you remember playing when you were a child. The object is to give baby word clues, using words in baby's vocabulary, then have baby guess what the object is. "I spy with my little eye something that is big, has a lot of hair, and barks when someone comes to the door." "I spy with my little eye something that is yellow, has a peel, monkeys eat them, and they taste sweet." The possibilities are endless. Add or subtract clues based on child's response. This is fun to play anyplace. Let older brothers and sisters participate in making up clues.

Silly Photo

Find an instant photo booth and think of some silly pictures you can take with baby. For example, kiss baby's nose, chew fingers, touch cheeks, and make silly faces. Put your change into the photo booth and make those silly pictures. Show them to your baby when they are finished, and when you get home, hang them up somewhere baby can see them often. Talk about them once in awhile, and as you do, tell baby how much fun you have when you are together, and how much you love him or her.

318

Have a Conversation

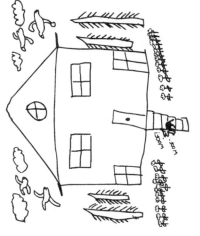

Babies take in every aspect of their environment every waking moment. Sometimes you may feel silly talking to baby when you can't even understand their response. But, be assured, they are learning how to communicate by listening to you! When you are out with baby, ask him to tell you what he sees. The answers can be silly or real. For example, if you see a dog barking, ask him why the dog is barking, and talk about the dog. Say things like, "I bet the dog is barking because the squirrel said he wouldn't play," "Maybe the dog is barking because he is scared of us," "The dog is talking to us, woof, woof, let's talk to him (then bark together)." If baby responds with any sound at all, make up what you might think they are trying to say to you. For example, baby says da, ba, ba, and you say, "You're right, the dog barks at the birds." You can even make up rhymes about the object you are talking about: "The dog, sits on his log, waiting for Mr. Frog." Be creative and they will learn humor from you too!

Edible Necklace

Materials
Cheerios or Fruit Loops
Thin shoelace with plastic tips

Getting ready for a car, boat, train, or plane trip? Go prepared with little packages of wrapped up food. Make it a special treat to reach into the surprise goodie bag. Make some edible necklaces to be included in the bag. String Cheerios or any other round cereal onto the shoe string and tie both ends together making a necklace. When baby is hungry, they simply reach down and bite a few Cheerios off. You may have to show them how to do this, so they don't think they are ruining a beautiful necklace. Wash the shoelaces afterwards and use them again.

320

Count Together

Kids love to count anything and every-thing. They will soon get used to counting from one to ten if you do it often enough. You can count stairs walked up, bites of cereal, pillows on the couch, cars on the road, chairs at a table, trees on a hike, waves at the ocean, rocks on the walkway, etc. Wherever you are, make counting a part of your life. Sing, clap, or make up rhymes with your numbers.

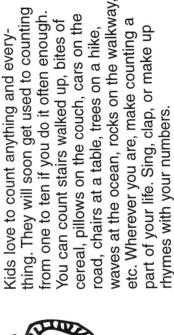

321

Baby-Sitting and Playgroups

Organizing a Playgroup

A playgroup is usually three children per one adult. It can be a group of children each with their parent, or one parent watching three children. The idea of the group is to let babies interact with each other and learn beginning social skills. If you and your child could benefit from interacting with other babies and mothers, here are some ideas on how to get a playgroup started:

- Ask your friends if they want to set a weekly date to get babies together.

- Make sure one parent isn't always doing the "baby-sitting." If so, he or she should be paid.

- If you don't have friends with small children, go to a local park and look for other children close in age. Other places to look are at day care centers, church, or put an ad in the local paper.

- Once you have a few people interested, get together and talk about parenting philosophies to make sure you feel comfortable with each other.

- Plan one month of play dates, then give it a try.

- Talk together for ten minutes after each playgroup about how the interaction went, what the children liked and disliked, etc.

322

Playgroup Leader's Responsibilities

- There should be no more than three children to one adult.
- Babies and toddlers are completely dependent on adults to meet their needs. They must always be supervised.
- Talk to children one-to-one. Let children initiate conversation, then respond to them. If they don't talk yet, speak to them describing what's going on around them.
- Be supportive of skills they are trying. Praise children often.
- Respond promptly to crying.
- Respect children's desire to carry around a favorite object.
- If children fight over a toy, adult should step in offering a like toy so each child can have one.

- Try to limit the use of the word "no" to safety issues.
- Greet each child with a warm smile.
- Model for children how to use words instead of being aggressive, i.e., "I want to go on the swing," instead of pushing the other child off.
- Have appropriate play area set up with activities planned.
- Set up a predictable routine to be followed each time.
- Provide healthful snacks frequently, especially liquids.

323

Parent Questionnaire

Make up a questionnaire for parents of children in the playgroup to fill out. Put this questionnaire in a folder that goes to the house where the playgroup is being held. Here are a few things the questionnaire should include:

- Emergency phone numbers: doctor, work number, alternate person to call for help.
- Food: likes, dislikes, allergies, and feeding schedule.
- Daily schedule with preferred nap times.
- Favorite toys or blanket.
- Favorite song.
- How to calm baby when crying.
- If baby is afraid of anything around the house (cat, dog).
- Names of brothers and sisters.

Put anything on the questionnaire that might make the relationship between playgroup leader and child more supportive of the child's needs. Make sure this folder is wherever the babies are. Good luck!

NAME _____
ADDRESS _____
PHONE _____
NAP TIME _____

LIKES _____
_____
DISLIKES _____
_____

324

Co-op Baby-Sitting

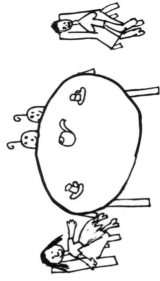

Co-op baby-sitting is different from a playgroup. A co-op is arranged as a baby-sitting option. It takes some organization, but can be very effective and successful. This is how it works. There is a list of people who belong to the co-op. When you need a baby-sitter, you can call the co-op list of names until you find someone who is available. There is a person who keeps track of everyone's hours. If you baby-sit three hours, then the co-op owes you three hours, so you don't exactly pay the person back who baby-sat for you. Co-op baby-sitting is generally done in the home of the person doing the baby-sitting, since most people involved also have children. The co-op can be as big or small as you like. It's a good opportunity to meet other parents and save money on baby-sitting at the same time. Take some time to brainstorm about how you could organize a co-op.

325

Hiring a Baby-Sitter

Here are some things to think about when hiring a baby-sitter:

- The first thing to think about is what you need most. Is it someone to do the housework so you can be with baby or someone to take care of baby?
- Make a list of what the job entails: baby-sitting, laundry, cooking, housework, etc.
- Word-of-mouth recommendations are best, but at any rate, check references. Putting an ad in the paper outlining job expectations is another possible source.
- Once the applicant is in front of you, explain all the things on your list that you would expect them to do. There is nothing worse than hiring someone who doesn't really want to do the job.
- Check if sitter has had first-aid and CPR classes. Make sure to leave emergency numbers as well as where you can be reached in an emergency.

- Since baby can't talk, have the sitter keep a journal of the day's events: how long baby napped, when they went to the bathroom, what they ate, if they went for a walk, what they played with, etc. If you want to make it easier, just make a worksheet and let them fill in the blanks.
- If you have doubts about the sitter's competence, have a friend or neighbor drop by unexpectedly to see how things are going. Or leave a tape recorder on to see how baby is being treated. It is your right as a parent to expect good care-taking.

326

What Can Babies Do?

When babies are small, group interactive activity doesn't exist, although babies will look at each other, respond to smiles, and interact in their own way. Put babies near each other so they can observe what's going on. Refer to the Floor Time, Language and Sound, and Movement chapters in this book for ideas on things to do with each baby, one at a time, within the group. As babies get older, they begin to play alongside each other. Later they begin to play together. You facilitate this journey by interacting with them and encouraging their play.

327

Calm Down

A great way to relax children after active play is a ball massage. Get a soft rubber ball or beach ball and have all the children lie on a carpeted floor or soft mattress. Gently roll the ball across their bodies, starting at their toes and rolling up to their chin. Then do each arm and leg separately. Do one child, then move on to the next. They will most likely giggle with anticipation of their turn to come. Say, "ball is rolling, rolling, rolling, and it's going to get you next!"

328

Toy Parade

Have a parade. If one of the babies can't crawl yet, march the parade around them. Each child holds a stuffed animal or favorite toy and marches around (or crawls) to the music. Scarves are also fun to wave overhead. Adults also participate, changing leaders every few minutes so everyone has a chance to direct the group. If kids are old enough, the leader can do other things to be followed like jumping, twirling, or kicking the legs up.

Little Rabbit Foo Foo

This old song is a favorite of young children who love to see the stuffed rabbit hopping around and getting scolded for bad behavior. They will giggle throughout and thoroughly enjoy waving their own fingers at the rabbit.

Little Rabbit Foo Foo, (stuffed rabbit hops around)
Hopping through the forest,
Scooping up the field mice, (rabbit pretends to scoop up a mouse)
And bopping them on the head. (rabbit bops mouse lightly on the head)
Down came the Good Fairy, (sprinkle hands down from above your head)
And she said: "Little Rabbit Foo Foo,

I don't want to see you (shaking pointer finger "no" in front of stuffed rabbit's nose)
Scooping up the field mice, (fairy scoops up field mice)
and bopping them on the head.
I'll give you two (or however many you want) more chances, (hold up number of fingers)
And if YOU misbehave, (all the kids wag their fingers)
I'll turn you into a frog."

330

Circle Time

Circle time is when all the children sit in a circle, tell stories, share something, sing songs, and enjoy being a group. It is a good idea to have a planned circle time when coordinating many children. Read a few stories and ask the children about the characters as you read, or say things not in the book like, "do you see the red cape? Where is it?" Children love animation, so be expressive with your voice. Then let each child share something they brought with them. If they are too young to share something, hold up something they brought and tell everyone what it is. It's fun to sing a few songs or dance to some music together. Finger puppets are also nice to tell stories with. If the kids are old enough, have them put together a small puppet show to perform when their parents pick them up. Circle time activities are endless. Remember not to make the children sit still for too long, as their attention spans are very short!

331

Bean Bag Games

There are so many things you can do with bean bags. First, when babies are small they can hold the bean bags and chew on them. As they get older, they can throw them in the air. Here are a few things to try with a group:

- **Bucket Catch:** someone throws a bean bag and the child tries to catch it in a bucket that they hold.

- **Crawl Race:** put the bean bag on each child's back and have them crawl around the room. Each time the bean bag falls off, someone puts it back on.

- **Hula Ring:** put a hula hoop on the floor and, beginning close to it, throw the bean bags in. Move farther and farther away as skill increases.

- **Pass the Bag:** sit in a circle with music playing. When the music is slow, pass the bean bag slowly. When the music is fast, pass faster. When the music stops, someone is left holding the bag. They get to stand up and do a quick dance.

See what other fun games you can come up with.

332

Obstacle Course

Everyone loves running around, crawling through tunnels, bouncing balls, and jumping up and down. Make simple obstacle courses for the children to go through, like running to the tree, then hopping to the rock, crawling to the flower, then clapping two times. After all the children have done one obstacle course a few times, change it around and do it again. Children will giggle as they watch each other running about. Try doing the course playing follow-the-leader with the leader making up what comes next.

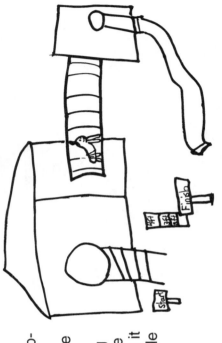

333

Freeze Frame

Most children are wonderful dancers. They just love to wiggle, turn, jump, and move to music. Turn on some music and tell the children to dance until the music stops. When the music stops, everyone freezes. They can march around, crawl around, whatever they like, but whenever the music stops, they stop. Join in the fun—it's good exercise!

334

Common Games

Here are some games you probably played in your childhood, but may have forgotten:

Simon Says: This is a simple copycat game. Start by saying, "Simon says touch your toes," and demonstrate touching your toes. Your child then copies you. Repeat with simple gestures. Then let the child be the leader. You can use your own names instead of Simon if you wish.

Hide and Seek: For young children, play hide and seek in a small space so you know where everyone is. Small children don't always get the concept that you shouldn't see them. They will be hiding out in the open, often curling up in a ball pretending not to be seen. Play along and say, "where is (child's name)?" even if you can see them.

Follow the Leader: One person leads, usually in a walking line. Everyone has to do what the leader does, and go wherever he or she goes.

Think of any other games you used to play, or better yet, ask your parents and see what they can remember!

335

Saying Good-Bye

No good-bye is said without some feeling! Tears don't make it a bad good-bye. After all, many adults cry in airports. Here are some ways to help good-byes go more smoothly:

1. Realize your child may react in a variety of ways: crying, sulking, thumb-sucking, defying adult requests, etc. This behavior is normal.

2. A gradual separation is best for young children. Leave them for a short amount of time, gradually working up to the full amount of time you intend to be away.

3. The child needs to feel safe in the new environment, so stay around awhile to explore together.

4. Let your child tell you how they feel. Listen and say back to them what you have heard. Then tell them you will miss them too, but will be back.

5. Leave something with your child that reminds them of you: a scarf, a glove, a set of house keys, an audio tape of your voice, etc.

6. Be honest. Don't say you'll be right back if you won't.

7. NEVER sneak out!

336

Food and Nutrition

Apricot and Apple Puree (4 months)

Ingredients
1/2 cup dried apricots
2 sweet apples (use less of these ingredients if you do not want to freeze leftovers)

Directions
Rinse the dried apricots, then cover with cold water and soak overnight. Simmer gently in the same water for about 25 minutes or until very soft and pulpy. Cool. In the meantime, peel and core apples. Cook the sliced apple in a little water or apple juice until it is soft. Puree the apricots and apples. Freeze leftovers in ice cube trays.

Note: If possible, buy dried fruit which has been naturally dried and is unsulfured. If fruit has been sulfur-dried, the fruit needs to be washed in hot water before use.

337

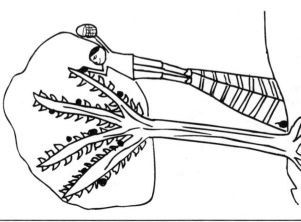

Vegetable Puree (4 months)

Ingredients
Any vegetable you would like

Directions
Peel and chop vegetable into small pieces. Steam or boil the pieces in as little water as possible until they are tender, then blend them with the leftover cooking liquid. Mash with a fork or put in food processor or blender.

Note: Here are some great tasting foods to add to your vegetable puree for babies 6 months and older: cottage cheese, plain yogurt, egg yolk, and wheat germ. To make a soup, just add extra milk, formula, or vegetable cooking water.

338

Vegetable Custard (6 months)

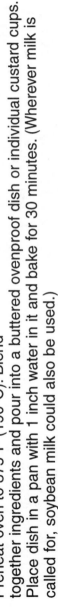

Ingredients

1/4 cup pureed vegetables (sweet potato,
    pumpkin, carrots, or squash)
1 egg yolk, beaten
1/4 cup milk or formula

Directions

Preheat oven to 375°F (190°C). Blend
together ingredients and pour into a buttered ovenproof dish or individual custard cups.
Place dish in a pan with 1 inch water in it and bake for 30 minutes. (Wherever milk is
called for, soybean milk could also be used.)

Wit & Wisdom: The best thing I ever did in the kitchen was
to clear out one whole drawer for my baby. I put plastic
cups, pans, bowls, spoons, and all sorts of safe gadgets in
it. My baby learned that it was the only drawer or cabinet in
the kitchen they could play in. I would change the contents
regularly to keep it interesting.

—Julia York, Walnut Creek, CA

339

Corn Cereal (8 months)

Ingredients

1/4 cup yellow cornmeal
1/4 cup cold water
2 teaspoons wheat germ
3/4 cup boiling water
1/4 cup nonfat dry milk (optional)

Directions

Mix together the cornmeal, cold water, and wheat germ. Add cornmeal mixture and nonfat dry milk to the boiling water. Stir constantly, bringing to a boil, then simmer for 2 minutes. Serve with pureed fruit.

Wit & Wisdom: Whenever I was baking, I would give my baby a cup of flour and a sifter. He would spend the whole hour I was cooking dumping that flour into the sifter, sifting it onto the waxed paper, then spooning it back into the sifter.

—*Sandra P., Detroit, MI*

340

Yogurt Plus (8 months)

Banana Yogurt: Mix a mashed banana with homemade yogurt.

Apple Yogurt: 3 tablespoons plain yogurt, 2 tablespoons applesauce. Place ingredients in a blender and puree. Any fruit puree may be used.

Carob Yogurt: 2 tablespoons plain yogurt, 1 teaspoon carob powder (8 months). Sprinkle carob over yogurt, mix, and serve.

Yogurt Ice: Mix yogurt with any fruit puree in season and pour into ice cube trays. Partially freeze, then add sticks, and freeze until firm. Keep a close eye on the sticks and take them away as soon as baby finishes.

Wheat Germ Breakfast: (Don't give wheat germ to babies under 6 months) 1 tablespoon wheat germ, 2 tablespoons plain yogurt, 1 teaspoon maple syrup, 1 tablespoon pureed raw apple or mashed banana. Mix all ingredients together and serve.

Wit & Wisdom: If you are visiting someone and have to feed baby but are afraid to ruin a good table, use aluminum foil as a placemat.

—Lorrayne B., Marietta, GA

341

Chocolate Dipped Fruit

Ingredients

Bananas, strawberries, cantaloupe
1/2 pound semisweet white or
   dark chocolate
1 tablespoon solid vegetable shortening
Toothpicks or skewers

Directions

Wash strawberries and pat dry with a paper towel. Peel bananas and cut cantaloupe into large chunks. In a double boiler over hot but not boiling water, melt chocolate and vegetable shortening, stirring carefully. Leave the bottom of the double boiler on the flame and take the top with the chocolate in it to your work surface and pour chocolate into a small bowl so baby can help you dip. If the chocolate begins to harden, return it to the heat. Stick a toothpick or skewer into each piece of fruit. Dip 2/3 of the fruit into the chocolate coating, letting the excess chocolate drip back into the pan. Chill fruit until chocolate is hardened.

Note: A good way to let the chocolate harden is to stick the toothpicks into a Styrofoam block covered with plastic wrap.

342

Egg in a Bun

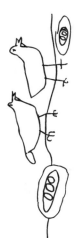

Ingredients

4 wheat hamburger buns
Soft butter or margarine
4 eggs

Salt and pepper
4 slices of cheese
Round cookie cutter

Directions

Preheat the oven to 350°F (180°C). Place all of the ingredients on a table. Using the cookie cutter, cut a round hole in the top half of the buns and remove the bun circles with a fork. Butter the insides of the buns and place them on a baking sheet. Break an egg into each hole and lightly sprinkle with salt and pepper. Bake in the oven for 20 minutes, then place the cheese slice over the bun. Bake 5 more minutes or until cheese is melted. Serve warm.

343

Wit & Wisdom: If ever an egg cracks on the floor, use a basting syringe to suck it up. It's much easier than using a cloth.

—Maria V., Orlando, FL

Baked Bread Sandwiches

Ingredients

Frozen loaf of white or wheat bread (the
   kind that has to rise)
Flour
Garlic salt
1/3 lb. hard salami, thinly sliced
1/4 lb. mortadella, thinly sliced
1/3 lb. ham, thinly sliced
1/3 lb. Swiss cheese, thinly sliced
1/3 lb. provolone cheese, thinly sliced
2 egg yolks, beaten

Directions

Thaw bread and let it rise, covered, in a
warm spot for one hour. Punch down and
knead with a small amount of flour. On a
floured surface, roll dough out into a 12 by
16 inch rectangle. Sprinkle with garlic salt.
Tear the meat into bite-sized pieces and
layer over the bread. Tear cheese into bite-
sized pieces and layer over meat. Layering
and rolling are good jobs for little hands.
Starting at the long end, roll up tightly in
jelly-roll fashion. Pinch ends together tightly
and curve roll to form a crescent. Brush
with beaten egg yolk. Place on cookie
sheet and let rest 20 minutes. Bake at
375°F (190°C) for 25 to 30 minutes or until
golden brown. Let rest a few minutes before
thinly slicing. Yield: 8 to 12 servings. This is
good to take
along on a
picnic and cut
when you get
there!

344

Grandma's Granola

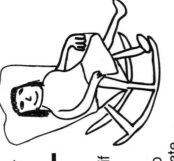

Ingredients
2 1/2 cups uncooked oats
1/2 cup coconut
1/2 cup almonds or seeds
(omit for children under 3)
1/2 cup bran or grapenuts
1/2 cup butter or margarine
1/2 cup honey
1/2 cup raisins or chopped dates

Directions
Put each ingredient in a cup or bowl for baby to pour into the main mixing bowl. With clean hands, mix together oats, coconut, almonds, and bran. Melt butter and honey and stir into dry ingredients. Spread evenly on a cookie tray. Bake at 300°F (150°C) for 20 minutes or until golden brown, stirring often. Stir in raisins or dates while granola cools. Let cool before storing in an airtight jar or container.

Wit & Wisdom:
Sometimes honey becomes crystallized if it is stored for a long time. Set in hot water or briefly microwave to return it to its liquid state.

—*Victoria R., Fort Worth, TX*

345

Cheese Pretzels

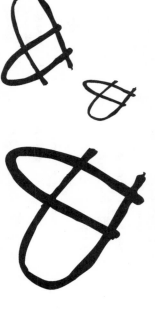

Ingredients
1 cup flour
2 tablespoons grated Parmesan cheese
1/2 teaspoon salt
1/2 cup butter or margarine
1 cup shredded sharp cheddar cheese
2 to 3 tablespoons cold water

Directions
Preheat oven to 425°F (215°C). In a large bowl, stir together flour, Parmesan cheese, and salt. Using a pastry blender or 2 knives, cut in butter until mixture resembles fine crumbs. Stir in cheddar cheese. Sprinkle water over flour mixture, 1 tablespoon at a time, stirring lightly with a fork until dough holds together. Shape dough into a ball, cut in half, then cut each half into 12 parts. Place each piece of dough on a lightly floured surface; roll back and forth with palms to make a strand. Shape into designs. Bake 12 minutes.

Note: A ball of extra dough, some flour, and a plastic knife go a long way!

Designer Pancakes

Ingredients
1 1/2 cups low-fat milk
4 tablespoons vegetable oil
2 eggs
2 teaspoons baking powder
1 1/2 cups flour
Oil or butter for frying

Directions
Put ingredients in a bowl and mix. Heat skillet over medium heat and add 2 tablespoons of oil. When a drop of water dances on the surface of the skillet you are ready to begin your art! Using a large spoon, make a design by dribbling the pancake mix into the skillet. Children are very good at making drip designs, just be sure their arms are clear of the skillet sides. Make sure that designs are small enough to fit inside a pancake. Cook design for 30 seconds. Pour 1/4 cup of the remaining batter on top of the design and wait until pancake has bubbles on it before turning it over (1 to 2 minutes). Turn pancake and brown the other side. Cover with syrup or jam and eat!

Note: Pour pancake or cupcake batter into a quart milk container for easy pouring.

347

Honey Lover's Chicken

Ingredients

4 whole boneless chicken breasts
1/2 cup melted butter or margarine
2 tablespoons flour
2 tablespoons prepared mustard
1/2 cup corn flake crumbs
1/2 cup yellow cornmeal
1 teaspoon salt
1/4 teaspoon paprika

Directions

Preheat the oven to 350°F (180°C). Remove the skin from the chicken breasts. Cut each boneless breast in half lengthwise. Blend flour and mustard into melted butter until smooth. Dip chicken pieces in butter mixture and coat well with crumbs and seasonings. Place in a shallow, foil-lined pan and drip remaining butter mixture on top. Bake 35 minutes or until tender. Dip into honey, or any other dip your child likes, and eat. Can also be refrigerated and taken for lunch.

Wit & Wisdom: Don't make special meals. Tell the child to take one bite to "try" the food, then if they don't like it they don't have to eat it (the child won't starve!). Eventually they will learn to like foods they didn't like at first.

—Laura Sullivan, Golden Valley, MN

348

Time Saving Trifle

Ingredients

1 pound cake
2 small packages instant vanilla pudding
4 cups fresh fruit
Non-dairy whipped topping
Fruit spread jam

Directions

Cut the pound cake in half lengthwise. Spread jam in between cake layers. Cut the cake into cubes. Set aside. Make the instant pudding. Prepare fruit by cutting it into small pieces. Layer in a glass dish, starting with 1/2 of the cake cubes, followed by 1/2 of the pudding, followed by 1/2 the fruit. Repeat, ending with fruit on top. Kids love to layer things, so clean those hands and design away. Refrigerate until serving. Top with whipped topping if desired.

Wit & Wisdom: When teaching children how to cook, repeat the directions many times and keep them simple. It also helps to show them how to do it once or twice before they start.

—Christina N., Augusta, ME

349

Ice Cream Cone Cakes

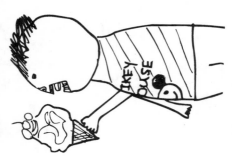

350

Ingredients
Flat bottomed
ice cream cones
Cake mix

Frosting mix
Cake decorations
Muffin pan

Directions
Prepare cake mix according to directions. Spoon the batter into the cones until they are two-thirds full. Place the cones in the muffin pan and bake at 350°F (180°C) for 12 to 15 minutes. When cool, frost and decorate.
Yield: 12 to 15 cupcakes.

Wit & Wisdom: There are all kinds of ways to make exciting ice cubes for parties. Fill ice cube trays with one or two berries, cover with warm water, and freeze overnight. Or, add food coloring or freeze fruit juice for ice cubes of a solid color.

—Louise J., Flagstaff, AZ

Gift Wrapped Sandwiches

Ingredients

12 oz. can chunk light tuna, packed in water, drained
1/3 cup mayonnaise (light or regular)
1/4 teaspoon salt
1 medium-size carrot
1/4 cup dark raisins
8 slices firm wheat bread

Directions

In a medium-size bowl, combine tuna, mayonnaise, and salt. Peel carrot and grate into the tuna mixture. Mix ingredients until well-blended, then stir in the raisins. With a rolling pin, roll one bread slice until flat and spread evenly with 1/4 cup tuna mixture. Roll bread with tuna mixture in a jelly-roll fashion. Repeat with remaining bread slices and tuna mixture. Wrap each rolled sandwich in plastic wrap, twisting ends with twist ties or colored ribbons. Or, cover each plastic wrapped sandwich roll with colored tissue paper, twist ends, and tie with ribbons. If not serving right away, keep sandwiches refrigerated or in a cooler. If children do not like tuna, try these sandwiches with thinly sliced meat or cheese. Yield: 8 servings.

Wit & Wisdom: The only sandwiches my daughter would eat for lunch were ones that were cut into shapes. The easiest shape was a butterfly. Just cut the sandwich diagonally and reverse the halves, spread with banana slices, raisins, peanut butter, cream cheese, or anything else they like.

—Jean M.,
Raleigh, NC

351

Development

The First Two Months, Big and Small Muscles

352

Things babies will do with big muscles:

- lift head for a moment or two
- search for something to suck
- hold on when falling
- turn head if breathing is obstructed
- does not control arm and leg movements

Things babies will do with small muscles:

- clench fists
- hold whatever is placed in their hands
- stare at objects
- stare at faces
- avoid brightness
- begin to coordinate eyes

Some other things babies do at this stage are eat frequently, wet a lot, hiccup, sneeze, sleep, yawn, and make interesting noises.

The First Two Months, Express and Think

353

Things babies will do to express themselves and learn about the world:

- cry
- might smile
- respond to being held
- become calmed by faces
- make eye contact
- believe they are the world, not separate from it

Things babies will do that show they're thinking:

- eyes follow faces and things as they move
- suck and chew things near their mouth
- listen

Three to Five Months, Big and Small Muscles

Things babies will do with *big muscles:*
- begin to control arms and legs
- lift and control head better when held upright
- kick their feet

Things babies will do with *small muscles:*
- hands still fisted, but relaxed some of the time
- arms reach for things with hands fisted as they swing and miss

Other things baby might do at this stage include sucking their fist and pulling your hair and ears!

354

Three to Five Months, Express and Think

Things babies will do to express themselves and learn about the world:

- use voice to express a variety of feelings
- realize hands and feet are part of their own body
- explore face with hands
- recognize you and other family members
- babble when talked to

Things babies will do that show they're thinking:

- look longer at things
- look from one thing to another
- hold object and move it around
- look for source of noises they hear
- cry less
- babble, coo, and gurgle to themselves and others

355

Six to Eight Months, Big and Small Muscles

Things babies will do with big muscles:

- roll from place to place
- move from back to stomach and back again
- have better head control
- creep forward and backward
- get to sitting position by rolling over

Things babies will do with small muscles:

- reach with one arm
- grab things within reach
- use thumb and forefinger in pincer grasp
- move things from hand to hand

356

Six to Eight Months, Express and Think

Things babies will do to express themselves and learn about the world:

- display a greater variety of feelings
- be more aware of body parts
- hear name and respond
- begin to see self as separate from the world
- prefer certain tastes to others
- want to feed self
- not welcome strange faces
- call out for help

- imitate others' vocal
  tones and inflection
  patterns
- use more sounds to
  express feelings
- see and grab for
  things wanted

Things babies will do that show they're
thinking:

- develop greater memory
- be alert during waking hours
- pick up object, then drop it and look for it

357

Nine to Eleven Months, Big and Small Muscles

358

Things babies will do with big muscles:

- crawl
- crawl with stiff legs
- crawl while holding something
- use furniture to pull self upright
- stand without help
- get stuck in standing position, unable to get down
- cruise along by holding onto furniture
- sit up alone

Things babies will do with small muscles:

- use thumb and forefinger to pick up small things
- use forefinger to point, touch, and poke

Nine to Eleven Months, Express and Think

Things babies will do to express themselves and learn about the world:

- fear separation
- grow very attached to important people in their life
- feed self
- drink from cup
- gain more interest in what's going on around them
- anticipate actions and activities

Things babies will do that show they're thinking:

- remember things and events from yesterday
- be able to concentrate
- want to know "what happens if...?"
- enjoy emptying and refilling
- listen to conversations

359

Twelve to Seventeen Months, Big and Small Muscles

Things babies will do with big muscles:

- stand without holding onto anything
- walk
- prefer to crawl sometimes
- climb up and down stairs
- might climb out of crib

Things babies will do with small muscles:

- undress self
- untie shoes
- use one hand more than the other

360

Twelve to Seventeen Months, Express and Think

Things babies will do to express themselves and learn about the world:

- show many emotions
- be fearful of strangers and unfamiliar
  places
- begin to know what is theirs and what
  isn't
- show affection
- respond to others' feelings
- want to cooperate, but not always
- become better at feeding self
- be able to help dress self
- follow simple requests

Things babies will do that show they're
thinking:

- find things that have been hidden
- imitate people
- explore different ways to solve problems
- use trial and error to figure things out
- be able to remember more
- realize words stand for things
- be able to say two to eight words
- use physical gestures to communicate

361

Eighteen to Twenty-Four Months, Big and Small Muscles

Things babies will do with big muscles:

- walk well
- walk fast
- fall less
- walk up stairs with help
- run, but not smoothly yet

Things babies will do with small muscles:

- feed themselves more successfully
- scribble with crayon or marker
- may untie shoelaces and unzip zippers

362

Eighteen to Twenty-Four Months, Express and Think

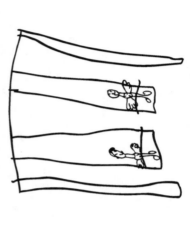

363

Things babies will do to express them-selves and learn about the world:

- pretend with adult, role play
- imitate what adult does
- enjoy doing "work" around the house
- have some bladder and bowel control
- desire to dress and undress themselves

Things babies will do that show they're thinking:

- think problems through before taking action
- use more and more words
- use words to get attention and say what they need and want lots of attention)

Two Years Old,
Big and Small Muscles

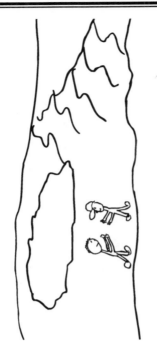

Things babies will do with big muscles:

- run smoothly, though still working on stopping and turning
- walk up and down stairs
- throw and kick a ball

Things babies will do with small muscles:

- turn pages of a book
- hold eating and drinking utensils
- spill less
- put on easy clothes
- use a paintbrush—with lots of drips

Two Years Old, Express and Think

Things babies will do to express themselves and learn about the world:

- be very proud of things accomplished
- say "no" even when they mean yes
- strive for independence—"me do it"
- try to understand "mine" and "yours"
- find it difficult to share

Things babies will do that show they're thinking:

- name some parts of body
- become skilled at problem-solving
- work two and three piece puzzles
- narrate what they are doing as they do it
- refer to themselves using their name
- speak two and three word sentences
- use "I," "me," and "you," but not always correctly

365

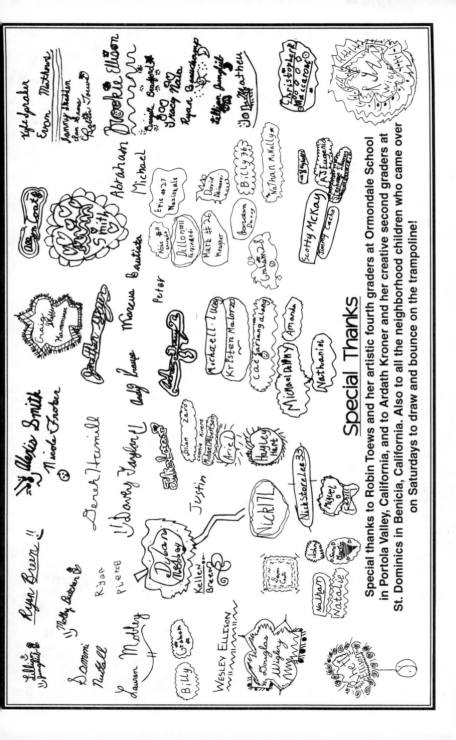

Special Thanks

Special thanks to Robin Toews and her artistic fourth graders at Ormondale School in Portola Valley, California, and to Ardath Kroner and her creative second graders at St. Dominics in Benicia, California. Also to all the neighborhood children who came over on Saturdays to draw and bounce on the trampoline!

About the Authors

Sheila Ellison has a BA in psychology from the University of Southern California, and is the creator and author of the very popular and successful '365' series of parenting books, including *365 Days of Creative Play, 365 Foods Kids Love to Eat,* and *365 Afterschool Activities.* She has also created and produced an instructional video on baby massage for new parents. The mother of four children, ages eleven, nine, seven, and five, she has recently completed national media tours presenting her ideas on successful parenting along with new products that make life with children easier.

Susan Ferdinandi is the Assistant Director and teacher at the Little School in Benicia, California. She holds a Bachelor of Arts degree from the University of Minnesota and is a member of the National Association for the Education of Young Children. Susan is the mother of two children, ages seven and five. She believes that caring for, playing with, and observing her children is her life's most important work.

Hungry For More Childcare Tips?
Don't Miss

365 Foods Kids Love to Eat

Fun, Nutritious and Kid-tested

by Shella Ellison and Judith Gray

"With its emphasis on variety, health, and simplicity, *365 Foods* is a boon to busy parents and hungry kids alike."
—*Parenting Magazine*

Written by the authors of *365 Days of Creative Play*, **365 Foods Kids Love To Eat** is a practical, easy-to-follow cookbook designed with kid's palates in mind.

416 pages, ISBN: 1-57071-030-9, $12.95

365 Afterschool Activities

TV-Free Fun Anytime for Kids Ages 7-12

by Shella Ellison and Judith Gray

"Sure to keep kids playing, imagining and creating all year long!"
—*Creative Classroom Magazine*

This Featured Selection of Children's Book-of-the-Month Club will let kids' imaginations soar during those valuable afterschool hours and beyond!

416 pages, ISBN: 1-57071-080-5, $12.95

To order this book or any other of our many publications, please contact your local bookseller, gift store, or call Sourcebooks at (708) 961-3900.
Thank you for your interest!

Also Available For Older Kids!

365 Days of Creative Play

For Children Two Years and Up

by Sheila Ellison and Judith Gray

365 Days of Creative Play is the essential guide to a wide variety of creative projects for young children.

"Activities that may work magic: projects that you can do with your kids, and even better, activities that they can do all by themselves."
—*Family Circle Magazine*

Written by the authors of *365 Afterschool Activities*, **365 Days of Creative Play** will encourage your child's imagination, growth, and problem solving skills.

384 pages, ISBN: 1-57071-029-5, $12.95

To order this book or any other of our many publications, please contact your local bookseller, gift store, or call Sourcebooks at (708) 961-3900. Thank you for your interest!